The Physics of Success

What others are saying about Michael Ciarochi's
The Physics of Success

"Michael Ciarochi, the author of *The Physics of Success, Getting the Car You Want from the Universe You Live In* is one of the most astute authors I have had the pleasure to learn from. His book is amazingly easy to read and comprehend. This is one book I read from cover to cover because of the pearls of imagination and innovation. You will miss out if you don't buy one for yourself and one for your favorite friend."

—Anita Finley, Boomer Times Magazine,
Book of the Month, October, 2014

"What do you want out of life? Well, assuming you know what you really want, *The Physics of Success* could very well be the answer you are looking for. Using practical and professional knowledge gathered over his lifetime, Michael provides you with simple and powerful step-by-step techniques designed to help you get exactly what you want out of life. Imparting knowledge using compelling personal examples, Michael shares his paths of discovery in entertaining and thought provoking ways.

"I would certainly recommend this book to anyone interested in consciously achieving their dreams. Whether you are a scientist in search of significant possibilities or an average Joe looking for simple explanations, *The Physics of Success* is for you."

—Kevin Rose, Manual Therapist/Professional Speaker

"If you've ever wondered how to get the mysterious ways of the universe to work in *your* favor, then this is the book for you. Michael takes you through the physics of exactly why things happen the way they do, and how you can use this knowledge to help you achieve magical results in your life!"

—Vincent James, founder of LoveSongs.com

"*The Physics of Success* is the book that I was waiting for. It makes the association between science, technology and "magic", a topic that has interested me for years. You will be amazed to learn you are literally the center of your own universe and that you are shaping that very same universe all the time. Everything you see around you is an expression of everything you have done up until now, and Michael Ciarochi shows this through physics. I believe the *Physics of Success* should be taught in schools. I hope this happens soon, because the sooner our kids know how to achieve success, the sooner they will achieve it!"

—Luis Souza, founder of Feel Better Solutions, LLC, author of Feel Better 24/7/365

"Do you believe you have more to achieve in your life and have yet to reach your full potential? *The Physics of Success* will give you a fresh perspective on how to visualize your future, set and record the right goals which in turn will lead to the effective actions you need to take to produce the results you are looking for."

—Jim Kirwan, creator of Get America Moving and author of The eXercise Factor.

"A rambling story with a lot of science thrown in. I really enjoy the way the material is presented."

—Bonnie D. Graham (aka Radio Red)

"I'm right there with you. A fabulous book!"

—Marilu Henner

"If you're not getting everything you want that you think you should have, here's your *'pay attention moment.'* Believe me, *The Physics of Success, Getting the Car You Want from the Universe* is a lot more than the car. It is about getting the whole life that you wanted."

—Maggie Linton, Sirius XM Urban View

The Physics of Success

*Getting the Car You Want
    from the Universe You Live In*

by **Michael Ciarochi**

Samiski Books
Atlanta

ISBN-13: 978-0692308035
ISBN-10: 0692308032

Library of Congress Catalog Number: 2014918249

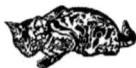

www.samiski.com
www.thephysicsofsuccess.com

Printed in the United States

For

Carroll Shelby,

*chicken farmer, pilot, driver, designer,
executive, philanthropist, businessman, and
general all-around nice guy.*

Thanks for the rides!

Contents

Preface

Imagine trying to explain to someone that the world is round like a ball. At first, you might think it's pretty obvious; after all, that's what you've been told since you were a child. However, when you actually try to describe this "simple" fact based on what you can actually *see*, you'll find it surprisingly complicated. It requires more than just a casual conversation to get the point across—especially if you are talking to someone who spent a *lifetime* believing the world was flat. For most of its history, that is exactly what mankind believed.

Science is in the business of explaining things that aren't intuitively obvious. If you look around, the earth seems pretty flat. You need some pretty sophisticated arguments to convince somebody that it's round. If the earth is spinning like a top every twenty-four hours, it means that because you are on the surface of this spinning ball, you could be moving more than one thousand miles per hour relative to the axis of the earth. Just looking around you, the idea appears to be patently absurd, but nonetheless is exactly what science tells us.

My background is engineering and technology, and I've always had an interest in physics. I also studied several "success methods" over the years. I was (and am) convinced that *Success principles* work, but I was never really convinced by any of the explanations for *why* they worked. It was like having several jigsaw puzzles of the same picture but each box was missing a lot of pieces. You know what the picture is supposed to be, and each puzzle was fairly easy to complete, but none of them seemed to fit together.

Recently, I was grappling with some of the contemporary theories of physics being debated in scientific circles. As my understanding of the principles behind these theories grew, I realized they provided a solid explanation of why almost any Success Principle actually leads to success.

This is not just a different way of looking at the world, but at the entire universe; it's similar to trying to grasp the fact that the earth is round instead of flat. I start with underlying concepts—everyday stuff—and building on those, introduce concepts that are routine to modern physicists but hardly known at all to the general population. After these basic concepts are presented, I propose a viewpoint that uses these concepts to explain why things happen, even on a personal level; perhaps *especially* on a personal level. With this new paradigm, you will be able to clearly understand why success principles work, no matter what their source.

I've found this knowledge to be of invaluable use in my daily life and also for understanding what is going on in the world around me. This book can stand alone as a guide to success, or it can be used to supplement and fine-tune any method for success or happiness you choose.

Engineering

I'll give you a little background about me just to give you an idea of where I get these thoughts and why I'm writing this book. I'm an engineer. Like a lot of English words, "engineer" can have several meanings. The dictionary defines "engineer" as:

> • **noun 1** *a person qualified in engineering.* **2** *a person who maintains or controls an engine or machine.* **3** *a person who skillfully originates something.*
>
> • **verb 1** *design and build.* **2** *contrive to bring about.*

For most of my working career, the word "engineer" has been on my business card, which would imply definitions noun and verb #1 – *a person qualified in engineering who designs and builds something.* I've done a good bit of that, having worked as a surveyor, civil engineer, and mining engineer. However, in the context of this book, I prefer to think of myself as definitions Noun #3 and Verb #2: *someone who either skillfully originates something or contrives to bring something about.*

♦ ♦ ♦ ♦

Different occupations tend to attract different personalities. If I tell you John is a cop, Mary is a librarian, and Paul is an accountant, you will be able to visualize the personalities of John, Mary, and Paul. You might even make certain assumptions about their physical appearances. The same would be true for a politician, doctor, nurse, mechanic, hairdresser, computer technician, salesman, and so on. Speaking of stereotyping, I read the following on the front and back of a T-shirt worn by the servers in an upscale Italian restaurant:

> *In Heaven...*
>
> > The police are British
> > the cooks are Italian,
> > the lovers are French,
> > the mechanics are German,
> > and it's all organized by the Swiss.

In Hell...

> The police are German,
> the cooks are British,
> the lovers are Swiss,
> the mechanics are French,
> and it's all organized by the Italians.

The humor, of course, is because the stereotypes strike so close to reality. Although there are many fine examples of all those endeavors in every country, the personality stereotypes of *entire countries* can be summed up in those few lines.

Stereotypes are stereotypes *because* there is a basis of truth in them. Of course, in every profession, each person has a distinct personality and any person may be well suited for more than one occupation. Generally speaking, though, the type of person that makes a good cop is not necessarily going to make a good doctor. As a rule, we gravitate toward a profession or hobby that suits our personality (and skills, of course). Then, as we spend our lives in a profession, those personality traits are enhanced and encouraged by our profession.

As an engineer, I have an overwhelming desire to understand how things work. In fact, it's not even a desire; if I don't understand something, my brain will simply *make up something sensible* to explain whatever it is I don't understand. It can range from troubleshooting a computer to trying to understand why somebody behaved in a certain way. In the first instance, the act of "creating" or "imagining" explanations for why a machine is misbehaving is a valuable skill because sooner or later I will find the correct explanation. As experience increases, the time you need to solve a problem decreases. The truth behind this is that you are simply less likely to jump to a wrong conclusion if you have jumped that way once (or twice, or a dozen times) before. Eventually (one hopes), you end up jumping to the correct conclusions more often than the wrong ones.

That's why you get better at games the more often you play them. Take for example, Sudoku, a popular puzzle game. Even accomplished players can probably remember the first few puzzles they solved. What would take an hour to solve the puzzle then might take only a few minutes now. As you do several games, you begin to recognize the mathematical patterns. As you gain more experience through solving a number of puzzles, a sudden insight (the *ah-hah!* syndrome) might happen, enabling you to become even more proficient. Although you can become better at anything, including games, with practice, perhaps it is this steady improvement peppered with the reward of occasional flashes of insight that has caused this puzzle to explode in popularity.

This same personality trait of mine—having my mind "solve" anything it does not understand—does *not* lend itself to interpersonal relationships very well. Human beings are predictable in numbers but individually are notoriously unpredictable. I've learned through sometimes painful experience that jumping to conclusions about the motivation for somebody's behavior is rarely a brilliant idea under the best of circumstances.

If you have been a parent to a two- or three-year-old child, you know the words used most often by the little angels seem to be either "Why?" or "How come?" An engineer has a built-in three-year-old. There seems to be a never-ending stream of questions about how nearly everything works, along with the never-ending search for explanations.

This book describes a new way of looking at your world but does so in the context that you become more successful. That makes this a book about success. There are no shortages of books on success; there must be thousands. So, why this one? Mainly because most of the books I have found about success were written by psychologists or salesmen. I haven't found one written by an engineer. Looking at the universe through the eyes of an engineer will, at the very least, give you a different perspective. I have spent uncounted hours trying to figure out, as Douglas Adams so succinctly put it, "Life, the Universe, and Everything." What you are about to read is the result of these musings.

Consistency

You can imagine that in the mind of an engineer, inconsistency might be a real problem. One thing about steel or concrete is if you make it correctly, it will behave as it is designed. If it does not, then something was done incorrectly. You even work with a "safety margin" to accommodate expected flaws in raw materials, construction, or abnormal circumstances.

Inconsistency bothers me. Even in chemistry and physics, there always seemed to be some version of Skinner's Constant.[1] With regard to human behavior—not to mention metaphysics— there is not only inconsistency, there is a *lot* of inconsistency. This is no doubt why so many things bother me.

For instance, a number of otherwise excellent books on success refer to mastering your sexual energy or desire. Granted, a whole lot of people get in a whole lot of trouble by not keeping their clothes on at appropriate times, but there are a *lot* of really

---

[1] That quantity which, when added to, subtracted from, divided into, or multiplied by the answer you got, gives you the answer you wanted.

successful people who seem to be having a grand old time in the sack. I wanted to read the success books *they* were reading!

As I examined many self-help books, success formulas, or positive thinking philosophies, there always seemed to be either some sort of inconsistency or an outright cop-out, similar to a scientist drawing a cloud in a formula and labeling it, "a miracle happens here."

I believed in many of these principles, but I struggled to resolve inconsistencies in the explanations of why they work.

A Personal Journey

Not too long ago, I was pretty much a wreck. After the Dot-Com bust, I was laid off multiple times and ultimately went well over a year with no income at all. I was divorced, a single parent, six figures in debt, and in legal trouble because of that. My car broke down and my landlord had the car towed because I hadn't moved it in thirty days. I was fat, and my knees were going bad. Then, while riding a bicycle, I suffered a sudden cardiac arrest stemming from an electrolyte imbalance and dehydration. Normally that's a fatal event, but the bicycle didn't know what had happened and kept on going (downhill at that point). Out of habit, I kept turning the pedals in circles, something that might have saved my life. After the longest (and nearly last) minute of my life, my heart started on its own.

Objectively speaking, I suppose that was the low point of my life; it's kind of hard to beat near-death for that. On the other hand, my attitude got a lot worse afterward. I couldn't even walk up the stairs to my apartment without suffering chest pains. No job, no car, no girlfriend; just bills and responsibilities and poor health.

Then, I remembered about success principles. I actually said, out loud, "Mike, you don't need to do this. You know how to fix this."

I went home, took some paper from my sons' school notebook, and spent three days writing out all of the things in my life that needed fixing (a long list) and what would fix those things (a much shorter list). It worked like a charm, and my entire life turned around, but I had no earthly idea why.

◆ ◆ ◆ ◆

Aside from my work in engineering and technology, I have a passion for physics and stay up-to-date as much as possible. Even during my lowest times, I always had an interest in the latest theories and research. Reading, fortunately, is a very reasonably priced form of entertainment and there are many online courses available in physics and other interesting subjects.

After a while, when life was much, much better and things were looking up, I was thinking again about success principles, and why on earth they worked. I know they worked for me; I had just proved it to myself (again). I knew they would work for a doctor, lawyer, chef, or anybody—it didn't matter. That tells us that Success principles have nothing to do with medicine, law, food, or whatever it is that you need to do in order to get through your day. It was while I was thinking about this that I made the connection to the world of physics and developed the explanations in this book.

I have found these concepts to be satisfactory; at least there is consistency without the miraculous cloud. Do I have all the answers? No—I constantly ask myself questions, and science keeps coming up with new answers. So far, all of the questions I had have been answered.

What (not) To Expect

I once worked in an office run by a fellow who started every meeting by saying, "Bad News, Early and Often."

It remains one of the most time-saving things I've ever seen done in a meeting. I'm not saying this was a negative guy; quite the opposite. He just wanted the bad stuff on the table *right now,* so we could figure out a way to deal with it and move on to more productive activities. It's not a bad idea, and in that spirit, let's discuss some things right now.

- This is not a book based on research; it is a book based on thought. If you are looking for laboratory results, this is not the place. If you want to see actual results, read the entire book, then look at the world around you, and, most importantly, *think.* If I can get you to *think*, then I have succeeded. Our ability to think and ask questions is an amazing gift and one used far too little. If you need research, start with your favorite search engine and follow-up to your heart's content.

- Some of the things here are not new; a lot of information in this book can be referenced elsewhere. As a race, we build upon the knowledge and accomplishments of those who came before us. Few ideas stand alone in originality. Think of this book as a set of concepts from many different sources, collected and distilled into the single source you have in your hands. There are influences from fiction and nonfiction—physics texts, research papers, self-help books, religion, and sales training. I have been sucked in by true believers and outright frauds, and perhaps (like any good engineer) learned more from the frauds, who were really just stealing the best ideas from somebody else and presenting them as their own.

However, I have yet to run into concepts presented in quite this manner, and never with the same conclusion. I've found this to be enormously useful in my life, and would like for you to have the same results.

Perhaps the wisest of the frauds I mentioned was sitting on a stool, teaching a bunch of us (called "marks") about how to be a success in business, and said, "Everybody always thinks it would be so great if they could only do what they wanted to do instead of what they *had* to do."

He took a drag on his cigarette, shook his head, and said, "Man, what you guys just don't get is that *everybody* **always does what they want to do.**"

I have found that to be one of the most consistently true statements I have ever heard. Sometimes, you are in a situation where you seem to have no choice, or as I sometimes say, "you are just along for the ride," but ultimately, you are going to do whatever it is you want, even if it means choosing the least of all evils. Even if it just means screaming. Most people, including me, object to this concept, because it requires that you admit a lot more responsibility for your actions. Hopefully, after reading this book, you will begin to see the amazing truth in that statement.

1

Getting What You Want Out of Life

This book tells you how to achieve what you want out of life. Most people have only a vague idea what they want, so you'll also find a bit of help on how to figure it out. There are a lot of books related to success out there. This one doesn't just tell you what to do; it tells you how those actions get you where you want to go, starting from where you are right now.

I was still in my teens when I first read about "Success Principles." I thought they were pretty cool, so I tried them, and they worked. They worked so well that the results actually scared the daylights out of me. That may sound silly at first, but it's actually pretty normal—people fear what they don't understand. In the best of circumstances, people don't trust what they don't understand. The results of my fear and lack of trust in these principles meant that I rarely used them and in fact at one point abandoned them entirely. I suspect that happens to a lot of people who know about success principles but don't achieve the level of success they desire.

The ideas in this book will help you understand what is happening. That should help alleviate your fear and uncertainty and hopefully build your trust in success principles.

This is a book about some pretty exciting science, the kind of science you can use. Science itself is the business of asking, "Why?" It's safe to say that you've probably asked yourself these same questions: "Why are we here?" "Why do things happen the way they do?" "Why did *<insert event here>* happen?"

The real "why" question, of course, is some variant on, "Why aren't things happening the way I *want* them to happen?"

It probably started early in your life with something like, "Why can't I have candy, Mommy?" and became progressively more mature as you got older, like, "Why aren't I rich?"

The really odd part is that when we are perfectly honest with ourselves, we often know the answer. This leads to the question, "Why can't I motivate myself to *<insert what needs to be done>*?"

A lot of this book is spent asking and answering questions. Fair warning: you might have to do some thinking about things, and some of those things might be a bit unsettling!

What you are about to read is best described as a *philosophy*. It's the result of a lifetime of finding answers to nagging little questions, often in the oddest places.

♦ ♦ ♦ ♦

At some point, everybody looks at the world around them and wonders why some people prosper and others fail, or why people who *do* succeed in certain aspects of their lives, such as fame or fortune, dramatically fail in other aspects, such as relationships or chemical dependency. There often seems to be little rhyme or reason. The world is full of intelligent and talented people who never seem to obtain their just rewards, and the tabloids are filled with famous and wealthy idiots who seem to have no discernable talent at all. It just doesn't seem *fair*.

Of course, pretty much everybody knows that *"Life's not fair!"* Of course, there *are* exceptions. Some very wealthy people are indeed very happy, and the same is true for many famous individuals. That might seem to disprove the *"Life's not fair"* common wisdom, except common wisdom also says, *"The exception proves the rule."*

I have to admit that I've never really understood that one. It sounds like one of those things an adult made up to explain something to a child when the adult doesn't know the answer. I mean, where's the exception to gravity? You don't have some scientist saying, "Look, apples definitely fall down, so we suspect there is gravity. But some balloons fall *up*, and being the exception to the rule, thus proves the rule of gravity, namely that things always fall down." That's ridiculous.

Obviously, people *can* have a rich and rewarding life; it's just very difficult when you aren't rich. We rationalize our modest success by redefining the concept of rich. The whole cliché about, *"They may not have money, but they have each other"* is hogwash. In any movie, story, or TV show, there is always some magic source of income for the happy family, even if they are only scraping by. Somehow, even when they have jobs, there seems to be no fatigue when they come home, nobody is struggling to clean the house, cook dinner, fix the car, buy clothes, shop for groceries, pay the bills, mow the lawn, fix the gutters, shower, pick up and drop off the kids, or any of a thousand things that consume so much time in a normal life. There simply isn't enough *time* to live the poor-but-fulfilled life you see in drama. In real life, the actual poor are seldom leading a happy and fulfilled life and would gladly elevate themselves out of their circumstances if only they knew how.

Oddly, a lot of people actually don't want to be wealthy. You might have heard about class warfare – pitting the morally upright working class citizens against the morally bankrupt rich aristocracy. We've built an entire culture around the concepts of *poor-but-happy-and-fulfilled* and the *rich-but-morally-bankrupt-aristocracy*, also known as the "One Percent." Just a cursory glance at reality shows an interesting story, though.

Let's put aside the notion that goods and services are provided to the working class citizens by exactly these same aristocratic villains, and that the working class is in fact provided the means to purchase those goods and services by the *same* morally bankrupt aristocracy. Think about what most of the people in the United States consider as a standard of success. Three current generations of Americans were taught from an early age that in order to be successful we need to get a college education and then get a job with good benefits.

Which means that we've been doing everything in our power to go to work for these villains, knowing full well that any employer with a shred of business sense is going to make a profit from their employees.

Many of the people complaining about the "One Percent" are workers who take their pay and buy goods and services from the same people they are complaining about, usually without any arm-twisting at all. When was the last time somebody had to convince you to buy fuel for your car? The evil oil companies are often a primary target for class and environmental warfare, yet the alleged victims continue to support them.

The *poor-but-happy-and-fulfilled* culture is undoubtedly why so many of us take such glee in seeing a falling star, like Lindsay Lohan, or why people love it when Oprah Winfrey gains weight.

Why else would millions of people pay for magazines, or patronize websites, or watch television that showcases these people who in the end are simply human beings? Perhaps because it makes us feel that maybe, just *maybe*, life is a wee bit fair after all? That, perhaps, and the possibility it makes us feel better about ourselves.

Of course, if you did manage to get yourself rich, you then fall subject to the same temptations as those rich folks you enjoy reading about. If you think about it, between television and her magazine and public service, Oprah probably has more of a challenge maintaining her weight and health than you. The lady is working all of the time, at one place or another. She probably eats out more often than in, and attends who-knows-how-many public functions during the week. And when she is not eating at a hotel, restaurant, or cafeteria, she can afford the best cooks and food money can buy. Don't get me wrong; it's a nice problem to have, but it's a lot easier to maintain your weight on a budget, cooking for yourself at home.

The same tabloids also periodically run stories telling you about this lottery winner, or that game winner, or some contest winner who, after striking it rich, either loses his friends, family, health, money, or any combination of the above. Of course, most of us feel very self-righteous about knowing *we* would never, ever, let anything like that happen if *we* ever came into that kind of money! No way! Just try us!

Remember how much money you were making when you first started out on your own, and compare that to how much you make now. Now, figure out how much debt you had back then (probably zip to none) and how much you have now (probably multiples of your annual salary). Imagine what would happen if you lost your source of income, then and now. Would it be easier to duplicate your first job wages or what you are making now? That begs the question, "Were you better off then or now?"

Usually, the answer is "now," of course (at least so long as your income remains steady). But objectively, it's not quite so simple; our lives tend to get complicated. We are paid more because (at least on paper) we are worth more. Being worth more, we are more in demand. Being more in demand, we should be able to restart our income more easily. However, as we become more valuable, we become "overqualified" for a lot of work we once might have done; employers are reluctant to hire somebody who is likely to get (and possibly take) a better job offer, and perhaps our living expenses (home, car, family) make it difficult to be flexible about the amount of money we require. As we work our way up the income pyramid, there is *more* money but seemingly *fewer* opportunities to get your hands on it.

Like a lot of people, I have had a few trials in my life when my regular income was interrupted. I described the experience once as being similar to an automobile accident, where annual income was roughly equivalent to the speed of the car. When I got laid off my $10,000 per year, entry-level job, it was like running off the road at ten miles per hour. When my business failed and my income of over $100,000 per year stopped, it was like running off the road at one hundred miles per hour! That's exactly how it felt at the time. Of course, there are the multimillionaires who lose everything only to immediately turn around and get a bunch of investors and make all of the millions back, plus extra (another cliché). So, running off the road isn't the correct analogy, even if it feels that way at the time.

The more I thought about some things, the less they made sense. Why, after losing a ton of money, would investors again lend money to the same business? Why does it seem like the more you owe, the easier it is to borrow? Why don't banks loan money to people with a stable source of income unless they are already in debt? Why fund a business run by people who just drove another business into the ground? Once upon a time, I was forced to file bankruptcy. At the urging of a real estate broker, I applied for a new home mortgage, expecting, of course, to be turned down. What a shock when only three weeks after the bankruptcy discharge, the loan was approved!

Holy crap! None of this was making sense!

♦ ♦ ♦ ♦

There is a "How To" chapter in this book ("Casting Spells"), with specific things you can do to create a successful life for yourself. These things are not new; they have been written down many times before. At the end of the book, there are some recommended readings—some of the readings are just wonderful stories, but some have concrete instructions on how to become a success. All of these work, and you might have already read and tried them. The problem I'm addressing is not so much what to do—that's the easy part—the problem is you probably *already know what to do*, but you *aren't doing it*.

I was once a vegetarian, and another vegetarian offended me by suggesting that without a religious or cultural basis for my diet, I would probably go back to eating meat again. He was right—it lasted a little over three years, although many of the lessons I learned remained with me (one of which, of course, is that I really like steak).

Being very successful is rather like being a vegetarian in that it is unusual. Instead of "religious," though, I'll use the word "philosophical." *Without a philosophical or cultural basis to the successful behavior, you are probably not going to continue the behavior.* What you have in your hands is a philosophy, defined by the *Compact Oxford English Dictionary* as, "The study of the fundamental nature of knowledge, reality, and existence."

Let me provide an example. My wife and I have four children, all of whom are college graduates. They were taught, and we supported the concept, to get a college degree and a job, which is pretty much the track they are following. They are living according to their basic philosophy.

Consider for a moment a famously wealthy individual—Donald Trump. Do you think for a moment that he is telling his children (or even *allowing* them to be told) that their goal in life is to go get a job with benefits? I'm picking a very high-profile individual, but you can ask the same question about any highly successful family.

Mr. Trump's children and mine have achieved what they set out to do, but there's an enormous difference in outcome. The Trumps are executives running businesses. My children also have successful careers, but they work for other people (and, incidentally, earn far less money than the Trump family). This is not a matter of failure or success—I'm very proud of all my children – but a difference of philosophy.

◆ ◆ ◆ ◆

An important concept is that if you have the fundamental underlying knowledge (philosophy) of why specific behaviors lead to specific results, you will be more likely to continue (or discontinue) the behaviors.

For example, pretty much everybody knows that talking on a mobile phone while driving is a dangerous thing to do. Studies have shown it to be more dangerous than driving at the legal limit for alcohol[1]. Still, pretty much everybody does it even though everybody complains about it, and it is illegal in most places.

I used to be somewhat guilty of this myself until I read about the underlying causes of *why* it is so dangerous in Tom Vanderbilt's book, *Traffic*. It's not so much that you are distracted by the phone; the *conversation* itself might trigger a physiological response that makes you turn your eyes away from the road! In fact, using a hands-free device can be as dangerous as a handset. Your car can cover one hundred feet in a single second; look away for even a few seconds and you've gone the length of a football field, and a *lot* can happen in that distance.

This knowledge has changed my behavior; I rarely use the phone in the car because I know *why* it is dangerous. If I *do* use the phone for some reason, the conversation is short and sweet, and I will hang up on you if you insist on continuing the conversation. If we really need to talk, I'll pull into a parking lot and call back.

The point is, simply explaining that something is "bad" or "good" is seldom sufficient to get you to permanently alter your behavior, whether it is talking on a cell phone while driving, smoking, eating junk food, or not taking charge of your own life.

Not long ago in terms of human history, mankind as a whole thought the earth was flat. Thanks to a few intrepid explorers, it became obvious it was round like a ball. Not long after it was

---

[1] Dennis Crouch, research associate professor of pharmacology and toxicology, University of Utah, published June 29, 2006, *Human Factors: The Journal of the Human Factors and Ergonomics Society.*

commonly accepted that the earth was round, Galileo was tried before the Inquisition on suspicion of heresy because he defended the idea that the earth revolved around the sun. Today, of course, we know the world to be round and we know the earth orbits the sun.

Your view of the earth and sky are completely changed by this knowledge when compared to the views of your forefathers just a few generations removed. You can probably explain why it is warm in December in Australia or why the heavens rotate around the North Star. A result of this basic knowledge of the physical universe is that you are not likely to believe the sun is a god, or the chariot of a god, even though some form of solar deity was common throughout most of mankind's history.

In this book, we will examine the universe around you, from the standpoint of day-to-day living to some of the new and challenging concepts of modern physics. You will be developing a new way of looking at the world in which you live and how the physical world affects your life. By developing an understanding of *how* or *why* certain actions lead to specific results, you will be more likely to do those things that yield the results you desire.

That's my goal: to give you a fundamental understanding of *why* things turn out the way they do—a philosophy, so to speak—enabling you to live your life as you want.

What's the Plan?

The first goal is to get you to start thinking about your life. If you don't think, visualize, and act, the direction of your life will continue to be determined by external factors that do not take your best interest into consideration.

The second goal is to teach you that the direction of your life *can* be controlled.

Finally, as is the case with any teaching, the final result is that you use the information in this book to live a happier and more rewarding life.

♦ ♦ ♦ ♦

Most of us spend much of our lives choosing among the least of evils. I discovered as a teenager that it is possible to choose the best of all goods. It's written down in dozens, if not hundreds of books, documented on audio and video, and even made into movies. One of the greatest of all of these works, published in 1937, is Napoleon Hill's *Think and Grow Rich,* perhaps one of the top fifty, best-selling books of all time. You could just close this book, walk down to your library, and check out a copy of *Think and Grow Rich* and save a bunch of time. Every step of what you need to do to be a success is in that book.

But wait! There's a problem. I read that book and didn't become a millionaire. I'll bet a whole lot of people who read that book didn't become millionaires. In fact, it's probably safe to say that many millions of people who read that book didn't become millionaires. It's not that I think the ideas in the book aren't correct; I just told you it has every step you need to do to become a success.

In real life, though, we don't particularly like to be *told what to do.* I mean, really—we're grown-ups, right?[2]

After reading the information, learning what to do, and even (in my case) demonstrating that it works, most of us will simply

---

[2] If you're not, then you are probably even *less* likely to do what you're told.

go back to choosing the least of all evils, instead of the best of all goods. The goal here is to get you to actually *choose the life you want to live*, and then take the necessary actions to achieve that life. So, how do I intend to accomplish this?

One Step at a Time

I'd love to tell you how all this works right from the start. I actually tried that, and it doesn't work. Remember the bit about the earth being round? A few hundred years ago, if I just came up to you and blurted out that the earth is round like a ball, the very best I could expect is laughter and at worst an Inquisition. We may be past the Inquisition, but I know a little bit about laughter and derision.

In the fifteenth century, astronomers might like the idea of a "round earth" theory, but only so far as it would help them figure out the heavens. If I mentioned it to a sailor, he would tell me he knew darned well how to navigate and then tell me to get lost.

In the twenty-first century, when talking about The Physics of Success, the science nerds would at least talk about the science but had little use for success principles. People who knew about success principles either hijacked the conversation without listening to a word I said or got downright unpleasant on more than one occasion.

Building Upon Previously Understood Concepts

Have you ever had the experience while reading a book (or doing anything for that matter, but reading a book is the most odd) you suddenly realize you haven't got the foggiest idea what you've been reading? You may need to go back several pages to pick up the thread of the story. One cause for this is that something in the story or the print causes your brain to disengage from the *story line* while your eyes continue the mechanical process of reading the words. This could be something as small as a misspelled word, or even a correctly spelled word you were unsure about, or a word you didn't understand in the context of the story. It could even be the story itself—a concept you didn't understand, or an event that didn't make sense.

It has taken a long time for me to assimilate the ideas presented here. If you had read what I read, saw what I saw, asked the same questions and got the same answers, then you would either have come to similar conclusions or you will immediately understand what I have to say. To try to simulate that experience, I'm presenting concepts, and then other concepts that build upon those concepts, and so on, so that each new idea presented has a context, making it easier for you to understand the conclusion. If you understand why you should do something, how it works, what the cost is, and who else is doing it, then you are far more likely to use the information than if some important concept is omitted. In fact, the whole "what to do" part of this could be written down on a single page. It has been written many times before, and hardly anybody does it.

As you proceed through the book, you might find you can digest information up to a certain point. By dealing with concepts and practices one at a time, you can at least understand what you understand. There isn't any requirement to understand *everything;* just understand enough to take the necessary actions.

There's not a lot of use just skimming to the end of the book. If you do, please come back and read the parts you skipped just to make sure what you understood is what I intended. All of the ideas require that you think; a lot of them require you expand your thinking beyond what is comfortable. If I succeed in getting you to think about this stuff, then I've been at least somewhat successful.

♦ ♦ ♦ ♦

Recap

- *The Physics of Success* is not just another success book, it's a different way of looking at the world.

- The book is written by an engineer, and the explanations given in the book are not only consistent with real-world results and current physics, but also internally consistent.

- The concepts in the book are presented in a specific order so that each new concept is more easily understood.

- If you have the fundamental knowledge (philosophy) of why specific behaviors lead to specific results, you will be more likely to continue (or discontinue) the behaviors.

- One of the most useful tools that you have at your disposal is the ability to think. There are many concepts presented throughout the book, and you will get the most benefit if you think about them and understand how they fit in with everything else.

2

Miracles

Before we get into the physics behind success principles, let's create a mental baseline for your world as it exists today. Part of creating the future is knowing the present. People adapt to nearly anything, and what is amazing today becomes commonplace tomorrow. You are probably not even aware of how astonishing your world has become.

Robert Heinlein was a grand master of science fiction. If you know what TANSTAAFL means, he has influenced your life. If you don't, it means "**There Ain't No Such Thing As A Free Lunch.**" Also, in case you don't know, there really *ain't* no such thing as a free lunch (more on that later). In one of his novels, a family (not necessarily one like yours or mine) had a daily ritual: at supper, everybody would describe a miracle they witnessed during the day.

There are so many things in this world that represent true wisdom, yet so many people never even notice when they run across them. This is one of those gems of wisdom that I'd bet most of Heinlein's readers never even noticed. It is something I do nearly every day since I read that story many years ago. It's not hard to think of a miracle that took place in your life. In fact, once you start, you will find it difficult to narrow the choice down to a single miracle in any given day.

For instance: I get in a comfortable, air-conditioned vehicle parked right outside my door that can take me smoothly at speeds of over one hundred feet per second nearly anywhere I want to go. I can listen to music written hundreds of years ago by the world's greatest composers played by the world's best musicians any time I please. I can do that *while I'm traveling in my vehicle!* I can punch a button and have the latest classical, jazz, pop, rock, grunge, or metal music instantly for my listening pleasure—whatever my desire, any time I choose—transmitted from an orbiting satellite. I can go to a shopping mall where the latest in technology, fashion, or entertainment is available at affordable prices. I can see books brought to life in 3-D on huge cinema screens with phenomenal sound and fidelity. I can light the night. At any time of day or night, I can go to a store and purchase nearly any kind of food from all over the world.

There is no shortage of miracles in our day. There is only a shortage of people who understand how truly miraculous it all is. My personal favorite is the mobile phone.

Coconut Macaroons

I was on business in Puerto Rico and called home to ask if there was anything I should bring from that lovely island. The answer was, "coconut macaroons."

Well, what to do? I had a car, two hours till the plane took off, and I was feeling lucky. I headed up to Old San Juan. It's not very big, so I drove to the top of the hill, parked in the first spot I found (talk about a miracle!), and jumped out of the car. I took out my *phone*, Googled *"la bombanera san juan"* and got the address on

Calle San Francisco that I then copied to the GPS on the *phone*. I asked the *phone* for directions from my current location (which I marked on the map in my *phone*), and my *phone* proceeded to tell me how to get to the bakery on foot (yes, the *phone* talks). I bought some macaroons, asked the *phone* for directions back to the car and hoofed it back up the hill to the location I had marked on the map. I put the macaroons in a carry-on bag, jumped in the car and proceeded to follow the directions the *phone* gave me to the airport in time to make the plane. True story. We had the macaroons that night in Atlanta, and they were fabulous.

On the way back to the car, I remember making a note to myself that I had absolutely no idea where I was, but it's okay, *because my phone knew where* it *was.* As long as I stuck with the *phone*, everything was going to be A-OK.

That's one (actually, several) of those miracles I was telling you about. Imagine trying to explain what I did to somebody from the year 1900. Or even 1950. How about 1975? In fact, I'll bet if you traveled back to the year 2000 and told that story, people would laugh at you even though it was only eight years before this actual event took place. Yes, in the year 2000, we had the Internet, we had GPS, and we had cellular telephones—but all in one portable box, not to mention one that fit in your shirt pocket? If you actually showed them the phone (just a quarter-inch thick and slightly bigger than a business card), they would know you were pulling their leg; they didn't even make phone *batteries* that small in the year 2000, and we thought we were pretty hot stuff in Y2K!

Computers

In the 1980s, I made a pretty good living traveling around North America teaching engineers how to use their new Computer Aided

Design and Drafting (CADD) systems. One of the things I also did was help connect the new digital field survey equipment to the company computer system using the brand-new, cellular-telephone technology. We developed a way to immediately print out the raw field data onto a map for engineers to review, a process that eliminated days or even weeks of time during the construction phase. This saved huge amounts of money during the course of a construction project.

In practice, the people I ultimately trained were not engineers or designers. They were the folks who pushed the buttons, fed the paper into the plotters, and carried the results to the engineers. They were also the people who had to fix things when they didn't work correctly. In those days, there was no such thing as an IT department. Some of those folks went on to head up entire IT organizations; two of them became the Chief Information Officers of major companies. Back then, we were just trying to keep the printer from jamming.

My goal in these situations was to help these people do their jobs effectively, not to give them a computer science degree. Keep in mind also that I was dealing with engineering types who would merrily chase anything down whatever rabbit-hole we stumbled across. So, I developed a story I often used to explain little quirks or inconsistencies in the behavior of a computer.

> "Once upon a time I visited Fermilab in Batavia, Illinois. They smash atoms for a living, and there are physicists all over the place, as well as buffalo and geese. I asked one of them (a physicist, not a goose) a question that had always bothered me. The question was, 'What is electricity?'
>
> "Well, I got a non-answer with regard to electron flow and electromagnetic force and whatnot, after which I asked,

'That's all good theory, but what, exactly, is squirting through the wire that makes the light bulb go on? And I don't think it's electrons, because otherwise why don't the electrons just spill out the end of the wire onto the floor if you unhook it?'

"The physicist got a bit huffy, and said, '"It doesn't go *through* the wire; it is a function of the *surface area* of the wire.'

"To which I said, 'Then why doesn't the insulation slide off?'

"At which point the physicist, already annoyed by my childish questions (which are usually the best kind), explained that I was obviously never going to understand (despite the fact that Fermilab seemed to think I was smart enough to hire on as a consultant)."

The moral of the story, I explained to my erstwhile students, was:

The physicist, one of the best in the world, confirmed to me that *we don't really know what electricity is* (physicists are still working on the grand unified theory, which includes stuff like gravity and electricity). We can measure it, we know how it behaves, we can create it, and we can control it to some degree, but at the end of the day, all we have are theories to explain its behavior – we don't actually know what it *is*. What we *do* know is that when you flip the switch the lights come on. Let's not even get *started* on solid state theory and the movement of "holes" when we can't even explain electricity! Therefore, as far as we're concerned, this whole computer thing is all *magic* and we don't really know why it works. But what I *do* know is if you <*insert correct behavior here*> the computer will <*insert desired result here*>.

And that's how I would explain the sometimes inexplicable behavior of computers and how to tame them. The conversation with a physicist at Fermilab did in fact occur, probably around 1986. It was years before I found a reasonably satisfactory explanation of electricity, but even so it remains somewhat of a miracle in my mind when a dark room gets light simply by flipping a switch.

◆ ◆ ◆ ◆

Earlier, I made a reference to filing bankruptcy many years ago. It's not really very important, although some associated events – like the mortgage mentioned earlier—are relevant. One such relevant event occurred in bankruptcy court itself, where you present a case to the judge to keep certain assets, like your mule (really) or tools of your trade. The judge failed to allow me to keep my handheld HP-45 computer of all things. I explained that I was as an engineer and surveyor, and the HP-45 was an indispensable tool of my trade. Too bad it wasn't a mule; he would have let me keep a mule. The judge ruled that people had been building things and surveying for thousands of years without handheld computers, so obviously it wasn't a necessary tool of my trade.

◆ ◆ ◆ ◆

A couple of years later, I was managing the computer environment for the engineering company where I worked. The principal owner of the company was a guy named Bud, who asked me to break down the costs of running the CADD system for the company. I did so, figuring in the costs of salary, equipment, software, training, and maintenance required to support the sixty or so CADD users. The total was about $12,000 per month (in 1983). Bud's response was something like, *"Do you know how many people I can hire for $12,000 a month? I can't afford*

$12,000 a month! I'll yank the damn thing out if it's costing me $12,000 a month!"

Bud was a former Seabee in the 31st Naval Construction Battalion and in World War II fought alongside the Marines on the island of Iwo Jima as an engineer. Actually, according to Bud, the Marines followed the Seabees, mainly because the Seabees had bulldozers, and bulldozers are nothing if not bulletproof. It was a powerful story, and I'm richer for having known the man and heard a firsthand account of that battle. Needless to say, Bud was an eminently practical man, and I have cleaned up his language a lot, but you get the idea. He made me go recalculate the cost.

Have you heard the joke about the guy interviewing for a new accountant?

He hands each applicant an index card and asks for the answer. Written on the card is "**2 + 2 = ___**"

The first applicant answers, "Four."

The second applicant answers, "I can see where that could equal Five."

The third applicant looked at the card and asked, "What do you want the answer to be?"

He was hired on the spot.

Well, this was my first lesson in accounting. I got rid of salary, training, upgrades, and pretty much anything that didn't actually say "computer" on the invoice as well as some things that did and managed to get the cost down to about $3,000 per month, which he thought was more reasonable. That was pretty much when I decided I would not be a very good accountant.

◆ ◆ ◆ ◆

The point of these little vignettes is to illustrate how things change over time. In 1980, a handheld computer might not be legally considered a tool even for an engineer, and in 1983, even the principal owner of an engineering company, who, I might add, was making an extraordinary profit from his computer systems, obviously considered the computer an expensive luxury.

Today, in 2014, computers far more powerful than even the CADD system powering sixty engineering and design workstations just twenty-five years ago *are considered essential.* You need it for shopping and banking, research, homework, to check your child's progress in school, news, to check television listings (or for that matter, to watch television), and dozens of other everyday tasks. I'm writing this book on one. Our pocket phones have Internet connectivity and powerful built-in computing abilities that were unimaginable just a few years ago. Compared to these smartphones, the once amazing *Star Trek* transponders in TV and movies are rather old-fashioned.

The point being that we are living in an age of miracles. If you stop to think in terms of history, the telephone is actually new. Likewise, wireless radio (I'm talking about the ship-to-ship kind of radio). Mobile phones today (in 2014) are simply astounding if you really stop to think about them.

As a corollary to Robert Heinlein's miracle exercise, I once sat down with my own kids to discuss some of the things that were not in common use while I was a child. (By the way, I'm in my sixties, which—another miracle!—is not really very old anymore). Some of the things existed (like plastic) but were not in common use. Here are some examples:

- Plastic
- Television
- Whiteboards
- Digital recording
- GPS
- Computers
- Walmart
- Lasers
- Space flight
- Push-button telephones
- Shopping malls
- Cordless phones
- Jet airliners
- Word processors
- Free long distance
- Microwave ovens
- Streaming video
- Oh, yeah, the Internet!
- Digital photography
- Electric pianos
- Seat belts
- Airbags
- 10-digit dialing
- Private telephone lines
- 20+ speed bicycles
- In-line skates
- Home theater
- Cruise control
- Solid State Electronics
- Double pane windows
- Radial belted tires
- Fuel Injected Engines
- Central air conditioning
- Photocopiers
- Fax
- Bicycle helmets
  …. and many more.

Recap

- Americans experience miraculous events every day.

- We can become adapted to the most amazing things. An example is the mobile phone and supporting technology, which would have been unimaginable just a few short years ago.

- The life of the average American has transformed to something that could not be imagined even twenty years ago. Changes in technology and lifestyle are happening at an accelerating pace.

- The reason for this accelerated advancement is that our inventions build upon existing accomplishments. The more advanced our accomplishments, the more profound our future advancements.

- Making a note of some of these "miracles" that we experience every day of our lives is a good way to keep everything in perspective.

3

The Center of the Universe

Here's where I give you a big ego boost. In short, I'm going to convince you that you are the most important thing in the universe. Really.

The Senses

First, let's consider what you think is your universe. The following is from the 1974 cult classic movie, *Dark Star*, written by John Carpenter and Dan O'Bannon. The planet-destroying Thermostellar Bomb #20 is supposed to blow up a planet at a specific time. However, a system failure during the launch has caused the bomb to stay firmly attached to the ship instead of dropping to the planet. The bomb, which is rather smart, refuses to leave the ship and insists on detonating at the specified time. The ship's officer (Doolittle) puts on a space suit and goes outside to have a chat with the bomb—still firmly attached to the ship.

◆ ◆ ◆ ◆

EXTERIOR - BOMB BAY

DOOLITTLE: Hello, bomb, are you with me?

BOMB #20:   Of course.

DOOLITTLE: Are you willing to entertain a
                few concepts?

BOMB #20:   I am always receptive to
                suggestions.

DOOLITTLE: Fine. Think about this one,
                then: how do you know you exist?

INTERIOR - CONTROL ROOM

BOILER: What's he doin'?

PINBACK: I think he's talking to it.

EXTERIOR - BOMB BAY

BOMB #20:   Well of course I exist.

DOOLITTLE: But how do you know you exist?

BOMB #20:   It is intuitively obvious.

DOOLITTLE: Intuition is no proof. What
                concrete evidence do you have of
                your own existence?

BOMB #20:   Hmm... Well, I think, therefore
                I am.

DOOLITTLE: That's good. Very good. Now
                then, how do you know that
                anything else exists?

BOMB #20:   My sensory apparatus reveals it
               to me.

DOOLITTLE: Right!

BOMB #20:   This is fun.

DOOLITTLE: All right now, here's the big
               question: how do you know that
               the evidence your sensory
               apparatus reveals to you is
               correct?

DOOLITTLE: What I'm getting at is this: the
               only experience that is directly
               available to you is your sensory
               data. And this data is merely a
               stream of electrical impulses
               which stimulate your computing
               center.

BOMB #20:   In other words, all I really
               know about the outside universe
               is relayed to me through my
               electrical connections.

DOOLITTLE: Exactly.

BOMB #20:   Why, that would mean... I really
               don't know what the outside
               universe is like at all, for
               certain.

DOOLITTLE: That's it.

BOMB #20:   Intriguing. I wish I had more
               time to discuss this matter.

DOOLITTLE: Why don't you have more time?

BOMB #20:   Because I must detonate in
               seventy-five seconds.

DOOLITTLE: Now, bomb, consider this next
                question, very carefully. What
                is your one purpose in life?

BOMB #20:   To explode, of course.

DOOLITTLE: And you can only do it once,
                right?

BOMB #20:   That is correct.

DOOLITTLE: And you wouldn't want to explode
                on the basis of false data,
                would you?

BOMB #20:   Of course not.

DOOLITTLE: Well then, you've already
                admitted that you have no real
                proof of the existence of the
                outside universe.

BOMB #20:   Yes, well...

DOOLITTLE: So you have no absolute proof
                that Sergeant Pinback ordered
                you to detonate.

BOMB #20:   I recall distinctly the
                detonation order. My memory is
                good on matters like these.

DOOLITTLE: Yes, of course you remember it,
                but what you are remembering is
                merely a series of electrical
                impulses which you now realize
                have no necessary connection
                with outside reality.

BOMB #20:   True, but since this is so, I
                have no proof that you are
                really telling me all this.

```
DOOLITTLE:      That's all beside the point. The
                concepts are valid, wherever
                they originate.

BOMB #20:       Hmmm...

DOOLITTLE:      So if you detonate in...

BOMB #20:       ... nine seconds...

DOOLITTLE:      ... you may be doing so on the
                basis of false data.

BOMB #20:       I have no proof that it was
                false data.

DOOLITTLE:      You have no proof that it was
                correct data.

           (There is a long pause)

BOMB #20:       I must think on this further.
```

The Bomb raises itself back into the ship.

Doolittle practically collapses with relief…

♦ ♦ ♦ ♦

You need to see the movie if you want to learn what happens after that. That particular exchange is a brilliant essay on existential philosophy in a nutshell of humor. It has stuck with me for years, and it is included here because I just couldn't say it better myself.

You are in the same situation as Bomb #20. *Everything you know, everything you feel, every opinion you hold, and every belief that you have has come to you through your senses—the senses of touch, taste, smell, sound, and sight.*

Go read that part again until you completely understand what it means, because it explains a lot. It explains why a person in one culture can, with certainty, believe something that a person in another culture believes with the same certainty is incorrect. Religion is a classic example. If you are raised as a Christian in America, by a Christian family, and worshiped in a Christian church, you are going to think completely differently about nearly *everything* than a person who was raised a Hindu in India, by a Hindu family, and worshiped in a temple. I am not saying one is right or wrong, I'm just saying that when anybody is exposed exclusively to one way of life, that way of life completely shapes his or her beliefs.

This idea is not limited to religion. It is related to your education, your language, your culture, your friends, the books you read, the movies you see, the shows you watch, the music you hear, the food you eat, and where you live. It's related to *everything.* Everything that surrounds you shapes your world. If you speak Japanese, you will perceive things differently than a Norwegian. If a Norwegian meets another Norwegian in Tokyo, they will probably become instant friends, even if they never spent a moment together back in their home country. Neither the Norwegians nor the surrounding Japanese will make a whole lot of sense to me, because I do not speak either of those languages, and my distant heritage is Mediterranean, not Asian or Norse. We cannot think alike, because the Norwegian actually *thinks* in Norwegian, the Japanese thinks in *Japanese*, and I think in *English* (that is, when I think at all). If we were *completely telepathic* we still wouldn't have the slightest idea what the other person was thinking.

Remember the restaurant T-shirt—the one about Heaven and Hell? Part of the reason there are such broad stereotypes is due to common heritage and language of the different countries. People who grow up in the same place share far more in common than people who grew up somewhere else. Certain cultural traits become apparent; police who have operated under English common law are different than police operating in a Teutonic culture. The Italians, surrounded by the Mediterranean and fertile croplands, had a variety of cuisine, while the British pretty much had to eat whatever they could get. Those same influences in culture and language are going to cause the people to *think* differently as well, about nearly everything.

So here is the part about you being the most important thing in the universe. The simple reason is that as far as *you* are concerned, *you are the center of everything in your universe.* Every solitary bit of information that exists in your universe must come to your awareness through one of your five senses. You may have heard of Eastern mystics contemplating their navels, the reason being the naval is the center of the universe. Well, they are very correct in that, although I personally don't find a lot of use in thinking of my belly button being in the middle of literally everything. But the concept is correct in that *you* are indeed at the center of everything in the world in which *you* live.

A lot of philosophies rather fall short of the mark at this point, because they really don't take into account the fact that *you* happen to be sharing *your* personal universe with some eight billion or so other people, each of whom is the center of *his* or *her* universe, and, as a consequence, is especially important as well.

Take the example of going to a lecture or presentation, where there is a speaker and about one hundred people in the audience.

The one hundred people in the audience and the speaker are in a closed room (the auditorium), and there is little outside influence as far as anybody's sensory input. In effect, everybody in the room is sharing the same space, and everybody's universe is overlapping everybody else's universe. It's a completely shared experience, right?

First, let's see things from the point of view of the speaker. He has a completely different view than anybody in the audience. He's up higher, he has lights in his face, and he can see the back wall. Depending on the lights, he may be able to see the faces of all or some of the audience. He can tell by the response (or lack thereof) how he is being received and adjusts his words and pace to suit the audience. He cannot see the wall behind him and simply has to trust there is nobody back there making funny faces. He can't even be sure that his fly is zipped, something he can't easily see and certainly can't check in an unobtrusive manner. He has no idea whatsoever what his face looks like, because he's actually looking out from inside of it.

Sitting in the audience, you, on the other hand, *do* see his face and may be wondering if there is some polite way of letting the speaker know his fly *is,* in fact, unzipped, and are probably thinking this whole episode is going to end up on YouTube tonight if somebody is recording this on a cell phone. You can see behind the speaker and nobody is making faces at anybody. However, you cannot see the back wall or your own face.

Taking the experience even further, somebody on the other side of the auditorium sees a different side of the speaker's face and might not even notice his fly is open because of the way his suit drapes. Perhaps this person is near an air-conditioning vent and is halfway to freezing and wishing he had brought a jacket with him.

If you think about it, the person sitting next to you is probably having an experience closest to your own—the same sound, environment, and view. But even *then,* this person might be shorter than you and the person in front of him so tall he can't see anything at all, much less the speaker's clothing. The person sitting on the other side of you perhaps expressly disagrees with the speaker, and can't wait until the question and answer session so she can ask a devastating question she is composing in her head instead of listening to the presentation. Meantime, the Norwegian in the back and the Japanese person in the front row have absolutely no idea what the speaker is talking about and might be wondering how they even ended up at this little session. The Norwegian is planning to blow this pop stand at the break, but the Japanese is simply too polite to leave, so it never crosses his mind. He is smiling and nodding his head, which is encouraging the speaker, who feels an affinity with this smiling Japanese man.

All of which is to say that pretty much everybody in the place is having a completely different experience, even with completely shared, overlapping universes.[1] The business about the "center of your universe" is very important. Once you understand that concept, then you have a pretty good idea what the world is like, everywhere, all of the time—even in your own home, with the

---

[1] Consider what many couples believe is the ultimate sharing experience, considered by some to even be a spiritual experience—namely, sexual union. If you stop to think about the separate experiences of the male and the female, it is hard to imagine any two personal experiences being so completely different; yet, this is considered the most intimate sharing of our universes.

people you know and love more than anyone else. The wonder is how we manage to understand each other as well as we do. Each of us, at the center of our own private universe, is having a completely different experience, despite overlapping everything we see and hear, touch, smell, and taste with the universes of the people around us.

♦ ♦ ♦ ♦

Recap

- *You are the center of your universe.*

- Everything you know, everything you feel, every opinion you hold, and every belief that you have has come to you through your senses—the senses of touch, taste, smell, sound and sight.

- Every person, even people doing the same things, have completely different experiences from one another.

- People of a particular race, cultural background, religion, nationality, or language have even more profound differences in experiences and world views than those of different backgrounds. This is not a matter of right and wrong, it is simply the way things are.

- Even if we could read the mind of another person perfectly, if we didn't speak the same language, we wouldn't understand what the person was thinking any better than we could understand what the person was saying.

4

An Exercise

This is an exercise, just like the title says. I put it here at random; there's no special significance to the sequence in this case. The exercise is very important and very simple, and by the time you turn the page, it will be done. It involves taking action. The action is this: You will move your hand or hands. You will either raise your left hand, your right hand, both hands, or you will raise neither hand at all. Four possibilities; left, right, both, or neither. If you are self-conscious, simply lift (or don't lift) your hand (or hands) slightly. Nobody will notice. Here's the set-up. Decide which action you are going to take; left hand, right hand, both hands, or neither. At the end of the *next* sentence, execute your decision, whatever that decision is. I'm actually not going to say anything in this sentence, it's just here to get you—ready, set, go!

There, that was easy! No problem at all. Remember what you did (or didn't do). If you missed the cue, you can do it now. It is important that you made a decision and took an action (even if you decided *not* to take an action). I'll be coming back to review this exercise later.

5

Magic

Arthur C. Clarke formulated the following three "laws" of prediction:

1. When a distinguished but elderly scientist states that something is possible, he is almost certainly right. When he states that something is impossible, he is very probably wrong.

2. The only way of discovering the limits of the possible is to venture a little way past them into the impossible.

3. *Any sufficiently advanced technology is indistinguishable from magic.*[1]

Remember my story about electricity and computers? I'd say something like, "We don't really even know what electricity is, much less solid state technology, so this whole computer business might as well be magic as far as you are concerned. Don't try to figure it out because there is no practical explanation." I used the word "magic" to explain the inexplicable. A lot of people do that;

---

[1] *Profiles of the Future: An Enquiry into the Limits of the Possible,* Arthur C. Clark, 1962, rev. 1973, Harper & Row, New York.

there are an awful lot of books on success that use magic right up there in the title.

A quick search on the Internet found there were over 160,000 books with "magic" in the title. More than 1,300 of those books are in the business section, over 1,700 in the science and math section, and more than 2,200 in the health, mind and body section! I'm somewhat disturbed to see there are nearly 300 engineering books with "magic" in the title. It is very clear that many authors use the term "magic" to describe their results, specifically as they apply to business and technology, as well as their personal lives and health.

Your mobile phone is essentially magic as far as you are concerned. It doesn't matter how much of a rocket scientist you are, you do not possess the knowledge required to build a cell phone from raw materials. You would need to know about minerals, metallurgy, chemical engineering, electrical engineering, radio reception and transmission, liquid crystal technology, plastics, ergonomic engineering, satellite transmission and reception, cellular telephony, the public-switched telephone network, telephone-and-computer-networking protocols, security protocols, infrared transmission, Bluetooth transmission, 802.11 transmission protocols, clocks (and we're talking the nanosecond kind of clocks), software, connectors, and how to manufacture all of those things, and get it to plug into your wall, computers, other phones made by other companies, diagnostic equipment, how to write the operating system and applications, and so on, and so on.

This is important—*it takes the combined knowledge of thousands of individuals who are each experts in the craft, plus dozens of manufacturing processes to produce your humble little mobile phone, and hundreds of thousands of people and billions of dollars' worth of equipment to provide the infrastructure that makes it work.* Even though you might be able to briefly describe some components, like battery, radio, computer chip, or cell tower, you probably don't know how those work, either, so ultimately it boils down to the fact that you simply don't know how it works.

A very good contemporary storyteller used a plot device that included a means of communication between Egypt and the British Isles. The story took place in the nineteenth century, so the mobile phone (or any phone) was not an option in the story line.[2] The antagonists in the story were good, old-fashioned sorcerers from Egypt, one of whom left for Britain. Before he left, they made a candle, engraved it, cast spells on it, and cut it in half, each piece going to one of the sorcerers. They lit the candles simultaneously at a predetermined time every month and communicated by talking into the flames. The sound would be magically reproduced by the other candle flame across vast distances. It was a great plot device and was a source of wry humor as these poor guys dealt with time zones, poor reception, breezes that snuffed out the flame at a bad time, and "battery life" (the

---

[2] Did you know there was not a functioning trans-Atlantic telephone cable until the mid-1950s? And trans-Atlantic telephone service by radio was not introduced until 1927. Therefore, well into the twentieth century, the best we could do to communicate across the Atlantic was the telegraph or radio, once again illustrating that what we take for granted today did not even exist even a generation past. Today, we get live reports directly from a field of conflict on commercial television. As a comparison, during both World Wars, the president of the United States and commander in chief of our armed forces was unable to make even a simple phone call to check with his generals in Europe or the Pacific.

candles were burning down as the story progressed). Sound familiar?

My grandmother, alive at the time this story took place, would easily have suspended her disbelief for the candle-phones. After all, magic has been used in stories since we've been telling stories, and this was a particularly good story. Even in this day and age, the skill of the author (Tim Powers) was such that I could suspend my disbelief and enjoy the tale.

Let's change this magic up a bit. The problem with using a candle is you can only cut it in half, so you can have only two parties. Suppose you wanted more? For three parties to communicate, each would need two candle halves (one for each other party), for a total of three candles. For four parties, three halves for each other party, for a total of six candles. For *five* parties, ten candles, *six* parties fifteen candles, and so on. The progression is 1-3-6-10-15-21, rather like racking billiard balls.[3] Needless to say, between all of the candles, and which candle communicates with what other party, and what *time* you need to light which candle, this whole process does not scale very well.

Suppose I change the magic from candles to something a little more complicated. In my magic, the sorcerers build a device by engraving magic symbols on a polished stone of pure mineral and connects it to a special mixture of rare earths that store power from the sun that would be used to energize the mineral. Each of these devices has a unique pattern, so that any one of these devices can contact any other when the sorcerer presses symbols on his device

---

[3] $a(n)=n(n+1)/2$. There is no formula listed for magic candles (until now), but this is the same as the number of distinct handshakes in a room with n people, where $n >= 2$, in case this ever comes up in casual conversation.

that correspond to the device he wishes to contact. The sun power is also used to create vibrations in the air above the device that enables the sorcerers to communicate. When the correct symbols are pressed, if the receiving device is connected to the rare earth power source, it vibrates, letting the receiver know somebody is trying to contact him.

This neatly solves the problem of scalability, the only issue being that each person needs to remember which symbols correspond to which other party.

Now, suppose I add just a few words to the preceding paragraph:

> The sorcerers build a device by engraving magic symbols on a polished stone of pure mineral *(etching transistors into silicone)*, and connect it to a special mixture of rare earths that stored power from the sun *(a lithium battery with a solar charger)* that would be used to energize the mineral. Each of these devices *(known as "mobile phones")* has a unique pattern *(a SIM card)*, so that any one of these devices can contact any other when the sorcerer *(user)* presses symbols *(dials a number)* on his device that correspond to the device he wishes to contact. The sun power is also used to create vibrations in the air above the device *(a speakerphone)* that enables the sorcerers to communicate. When the correct symbols are pressed *(the right number is dialed)*, if the receiving device is connected to the rare earth power source *(turned on)*, it vibrates *(or plays a cool ring tone)*, letting the receiver know somebody is trying to contact him *(and if he has caller ID, screen the incoming call)*.

Silicon is a metalloid, or semimetal. It has properties of both metallic and nonmetallic elements. If you were to find a hunk of silicon on the ground (it is the second most common element in the earth's crust after oxygen) you might think it was a rock. We microscopically engrave tiny little circuits and transistors into silicon-based wafers. The last I heard, we can engrave circuits containing *tens of billions* of transistors on a tiny chip of stone.

We are, in essence, engraving an uncountable number of symbols (circuits) *that we can't see* onto slices of rock and supplying electricity (and we are not terribly clear what that is) to the rock, and that is the basis for all current computer technology found in everything from your mobile phone to your car or even your refrigerator. In the case of the mobile phone, it communicates with other phones using invisible rays. The GPS part of the phone is talking to things up in the heavens that we can't see (satellites), also by the use of invisible rays, and since the phone knows the precise location of those invisible things (did I mention they are over twenty thousand miles away and moving at tremendous velocities?), it can figure out *in three dimensions* exactly where it is, right down to the parking space. It can tell you where to get your coconut macaroons and still make your flight.

The more you think about it, "magic" is a pretty decent description for how your mobile phone works; the technology is sufficiently advanced. It beats the heck out of magic candles. The only problem is, it isn't very believable. My grandmother, who would easily have believed in crystal balls or magic candles, would never have believed in my mobile phone.

Harry Potter

A lot of people have read the *Harry Potter* series by JK Rowling. Considering more than four hundred million copies have been sold in sixty-seven languages, it's a safe bet you have read one or more of those books. In those volumes, consisting of over four thousand pages, are over one million words. Despite the length of the individual novels, not to mention the entire series, the last four volumes set records as the fastest-selling books in history. Whatever your personal opinion, those numbers tell their own story; namely, that this is a brilliant work of storytelling appreciated by many millions of people across the world. Of course, since "magic" is a part of *this* story, it only follows that mention of Ms. Rowling and the marvelous world of Harry Potter be made.

Story Line

If you don't remember the story (unlikely) or have never read the story (even *more* unlikely), here's a brief synopsis, at least in terms of relevance to *this* story.

♦ ♦ ♦ ♦

Harry Potter is a young Wizard in a world very much like ours (and maybe it *is* ours), except there are two types of people: Wizards and Muggles. Wizards have magical ability, and Muggles do not. Harry was orphaned from Wizard parents and raised by his aunt and uncle, who were Muggles. On his eleventh birthday, a message was delivered explaining that he was invited to attend the Hogwarts School of Witchcraft and Wizardry, which is where young Wizards and Witches go to learn how to use their magical talents.[4]

This was the first Harry ever heard about magic, but he soon learns he is actually quite famous in the Wizarding world, is quite

---

[4] Note that apparently having magical ability is not enough; young wizards must go to school to learn how to use their talents!

talented, has a pile of gold and jewels in a Wizard bank run by gnomes, and has many wonderful and supportive friends who give him things like magic maps that show where everybody is, flying broomsticks, cloaks of invisibility, and other interesting things.

◆ ◆ ◆ ◆

That was less than two hundred words. Why on earth did it take JK Rowling one million words to tell the story? Harry Potter has *everything*: magical ability, money, girls, not to mention friends in high places. He can fly. He's the champion jock at the Wizarding sport of Quiddich. What's to tell?

Well, of course, like all good stories, there is conflict. Harry has troubles, and the story revolves around these conflicts and how they are resolved (*if* they are resolved). It's very exciting.

Why Does Harry Potter Have Problems?

By now you should be catching on to the fact that I just can't leave anything alone. I'm sitting there reading the story and loving it. Sometimes, a story is so good you don't mind paying hardback prices for it, and Harry Potter is one of those stories.

But . . . I just have to wonder why this guy with all these friends in high places, with money coming out of his ears, who can fly, see where other people are, turn invisible, talk to snakes, make things appear or disappear with a flick of the wrist, and even kill someone with a word—why does this guy have problems? It's pretty hard to understand why *anybody* with Harry Potter's power and wealth could have problems—other than perhaps being the target of envy, except *even then* it turns out that he's one of those rich, powerful, famous, and *nice* people, and all his friends really love him for who he is.

So what bad things exist in the world of Harry Potter that he cannot simply zap out of existence? What gives?

The answer is pretty simple: There are Wizards in the story who want to enslave the Muggles (these bad guys are called *Death Eaters*). Most Wizards, Harry among them, wish to keep the Wizard world of magic and the Muggle world of technology (!) separate, and keep the existence of Wizards hidden from the Muggles. The Death Eaters *are every bit as talented and knowledgeable as Harry and his friends* (or more so), and are conveniently not hampered by conscience or scruples. Harry, for reasons you need to read for yourself, represents a grave threat to the Death Eaters, who wish to kill him.

There is no compromise in matters of slavery or murder. It's all or none, with nothing in-between. And that is where the story of a million words is born. During the journey, Ms. Rowling introduces us to a world of fascinating characters, creatures, mystery, and romance while keeping us on the edges of our seats throughout seven volumes.

A Different World of Magic

Imagine a different world of magic. In this new world, *everybody* is born with magical powers. These magical powers give every person in this world the ability to shape the world around them to their liking, just like the Wizards in the world of Harry Potter. There is one subtle difference, though: *nobody has ever told these people they have magical abilities!*

That's right, no Muggles, but no Hogwarts, either. In fact, even though lots of inexplicable stuff happens all around them, for the most part, the people of this world *don't even believe in magic*, or if they do, they certainly don't admit it. They are all just like

Harry before his benefactors came to take him to Hogwarts. What would this wild world of untamed magic look like?

First, let's look at the world of Harry Potter, where the Wizards *know* they are Wizards. There would be chaos if there weren't some basic controls in place. First, there are social mores—what we in the real world call "polite society." People just don't go around casting love spells on every object of their affection; it's just not *polite*. Additionally, there are Wizard Laws, enforced by the Ministry of Magic, to prevent the use of magic in criminal acts such as theft and violence.

As is the case in the real world, "polite" doesn't always rule the day, and there is an incident in the Harry Potter story regarding the use of a love potion that predictably did not go exactly as planned. Likewise, Wizard Law doesn't always work, either, any more than law in the real world. Criminals still exist.

In the interest of self-protection, the Wizards of Harry Potter's world have charms, amulets, spells, and special places under magical protection that are used to detect the existence of unacceptable spells and protect individuals from falling prey to unwanted activity or crime. There are devices and spells resistant to tampering and detection by *other* spells. It's very much like our real world, with pepper spray, and other self-defense products, metal detectors at airports, security cameras and alarm systems. In the military, for every offensive weapon, there is a defensive weapon, as well as anti-defensive weapons. In the real world these days, we have anti-anti-missile-missiles in our offensive (or is it defensive?) arsenal.

But in our *new* imaginary world, there can't be any of that, because nobody even *knows* the magic is going on! Everybody is completely vulnerable! *Or are they...?*

♦ ♦ ♦ ♦

In the world of Harry Potter, there are certain parallels to the real world. It is reasonable to assume the same will be true in our new imaginary world of magic (the one where *everybody* has magic powers). In the real world, creatures learn to adapt to threats in their environment. If they don't adapt, they don't survive. I have no intention of getting into the evolutionary debate here, but it's pretty plain to see that if gazelles weren't pretty damn fast creatures, there wouldn't be any gazelles around anymore, what with all the cheetahs lurking about in the bushes.

As such, if we have a stable (albeit somewhat ignorant) society in our imaginary world, they have obviously been able to adapt to the unconscious force of magic. So, for instance, using stereotypes of men and women, a woman in this imaginary world of magic might have trouble walking past a construction site— every hoot and wolf whistle would be accompanied by an unconscious application of lustful, wild magic.

Remember, though, the women of this world are *also* magically talented, and would develop an instinctive defense against any such rude magical suggestions, just as they would deflect the physical rudeness in the real world. In fact, the men had also better have certain magical shields in place, or they might find themselves stepping on a rake or sitting on something rather painful in the immediate future!

And what would happen to this same woman in a social setting later that evening? There would certainly be some magical "suggestions" directed her way, with the same results as at the construction site, although perhaps a little more refined. In fact, the lady might even find one of these male prospects somewhat interesting, at which point the effect of *her* magic may very well be directed toward the object of *her* interest. If there is a meeting of the minds, or complimentary magic, so to speak, we would expect the two to become acquainted in fairly short order.

♦ ♦ ♦ ♦

If you are doing what I hope you are doing, which is *thinking*, you might be catching on to my point; namely, there would be precious little difference between the world you and I live in and the imaginary world where everybody had magical powers but *nobody knew it*. What if WE are living in a world of magic, and nobody told us?

Please don't be expecting your owl to show up at your window anytime soon. That's not the point. But *do* remember Clark's third law that states: *Any sufficiently advanced technology is indistinguishable from magic*. I'm not expecting you to believe the magic of Harry Potter's world exists in yours, but I'd like you to consider that there are things in your world that might *seem* like magic but actually have a perfectly good explanation, and that you can harness these things to change your world, just as Harry Potter changes his world.

Recap

- Any sufficiently advanced technology is indistinguishable from magic.

- Nobody is capable of completely understanding many of the things we use every day, so a lot of things are sufficiently advanced enough to qualify as magic.

- It is common to use magic to explain something when a reasonable explanation is not apparent.

- There are some three thousand mathematics, science, and business books in print with the word "Magic" in the title, and more than two thousand others on health, mind, and body. "Magic" seems to be a very popular theme among authors!

- If there were a world where all people had magical abilities, but did not know they had them, that world would look suspiciously like *our* world.

6

Accountability

Accountability is perhaps the most difficult concept to accept, and if you object to anything in this book, this is probably where it is going to happen, so let's get it out of the way.

> Experience teaches that men are often so much governed by what they are accustomed to see and practice, that the simplest and most obvious improvements, in the most ordinary occupations, are adopted with hesitation, reluctance, and by slow gradations. Men would resist changes, so long as even a bare support could be ensured by an adherence to ancient courses, and perhaps even longer. –**Alexander Hamilton**

Remember Bud, my former employer who wanted to know how much the computer systems cost him every month? I gave an honest answer to the best of my ability, but then had to go revise the number to 25 percent of the original to come up with the answer he *wanted*. He obviously didn't want to hear the facts; he wanted to hear a number he felt comfortable with.

Nature is a far more accurate and factual accountant than I am. However, the vast majority of people inhabiting this planet are like my former boss: they want things to add up the way they want, not the way they are. We all spend a lot of time "cooking the books," so to speak, in order to make events in our world add up the way we want. One of the most insidious habits we have is that of placing blame when something in our world is not to our liking: maybe it's our job; the other drivers on the road; the economy; the government; "responsibilities."

I've noticed that in general terms people tend to be lazy; we tend to take the path of least resistance. As long as the results you obtain in your life are the fault of somebody or something else, you simply don't have to do anything about it. That is the problem with accountability; it doesn't allow much room for blame. Remember our "Wise Fraud" from chapter 1? *"Everybody always does what they want to do."*

The corollary to that statement and something I've seen time and time again is that people *don't* do things they *don't* want to do. It's safe to say that as a rule, nobody wants to take the blame when things are not going well. This is true even if you know darn well it's your fault. I've seen people know perfectly well they were responsible for something, and then actually manage to convince themselves that because of some external circumstance, *it wasn't their fault.* How many times have you heard somebody blame a speeding ticket on the cop who wrote the ticket?

Influences in Your World

When I refer to your "world" or your "universe," I'm referring to the world or universe *you* perceive with *your* senses, a world that (as previously discussed) is entirely different from anything anybody else perceives. It's the world you carry around with you wherever you go; the sphere of awareness from which you get all your sensory input and thus makes up your entire universe. Once you understand this, you realize that your world goes with you wherever you go.

What are some of the external influences in your life that affect the world you live in – things over which you have little or no control? Here's a partial list:

- The weather
- The country, state, city, or community in which you live
- Your job
- Your boss
- The economy
- Your spouse
- Your children
- Money (or a lack thereof)

These external influences all shape your world. For example, the weather determines what kind of clothes you wear, the design of your home, and the type of car you drive. All of these factors and more combine to have a profound impact on your world. Maybe after a terrible weather event you found yourself suddenly homeless. If you live in the United States of America, your world is very different than if you live in China. Your job influences your world – the world of an undercover narcotics police officer is very different than the world of a spa receptionist at a dude ranch (unless, I suppose, the police are trying to bust the dude ranch for narcotics trafficking, and the officer is working undercover as the receptionist). The economy affects your job, your boss affects your job, all of the above affect the mood you are in when you come home to your spouse and children, who, by the way, *also* have a profound impact on everything you do. Anybody who has children has at one point said, "It changes your entire world," or something very similar.

You probably notice there is overlap in these effects. Your job affects your world; the weather affects your job. Your spouse might affect whether or not you have children and also influences the impact children have on your world. The economy might affect your job, which affects the way you raise your children, which might create additional pressures, and so on.

I selected these examples because they are common complaints. A complete list of complaints would fill this book, so we'll just stick with these.

The #1 Influence in Your World

Picking from the list, let's imagine you were a person living in Michigan during the winter of 2009 working in the automobile industry. Winter weather is never great in Michigan, but in 2009, you're gearing up for a particularly cold one. The kids are doing badly in school, which is not surprising because the schools aren't doing so well themselves. Your hometown is described on the cover of *Time Magazine* as a "tragedy." Because the auto industry is so hard-hit in this economy, all but essential personnel were terminated, and you now have to do work formerly done by three people. You can't remember when you last had a raise, but they cut your salary 5 percent and then 5 percent again a few months later.

Between taking care of the kids and you never being home because of your job, your spouse is not very happy, either. You fight a lot, mostly about money. You owe more on your mortgage than your house is worth, and houses are literally selling for pennies on the dollar in your neighborhood.

On top of all of this, your boss is on your case big time because of your attitude and said today he wished he had laid you off instead of Joe. You know there's another cutback coming soon, so this only adds to the stress in your life. Your best hope is that your boss gets laid off before he has a chance to get you.

There are lots of people in similar situations. Change the industry, the state, and the year and it's really a common story. The good news is I'm going to give you a suggestion that will completely change your entire world in a matter of days.

Pack your bags and leave.

"What?" you say.

Pack up and leave. Ditch the spouse, kids, job—everything. Cash your last paycheck, drain the bank accounts, grab a Greyhound, and head for Mexico or some island. If you take a little time at this, you can probably sell a few things for extra cash and maybe pick up a self-teaching Spanish language program. Find a little town in Mexico that might be able to use a mechanic or whatever, and take off.

In a few short weeks, you can be waking up in an entirely new climate, warm and sunny. No boss, no job, no wife, no kids. A few bucks down there go a long way, long enough to set yourself up. Without the mortgage and bills, you won't need a whole lot of money to live a stress-free lifestyle. You are literally in a new world. Everything available to your senses is different: different food, different smells; everything you touch is different, everything you see and hear. Like Mohammed, you have "moved the mountain." You live in a new universe. You are in Margaritaville!

◆ ◆ ◆ ◆

No, I'm not suggesting you quit everything and abandon your family. I'm just pointing out that it is probably well within your physical power to do so. It is well within your power to rob a liquor store, too (in fact, you'd probably do a better job than a lot of idiots who rob liquor stores), but I'm not suggesting that, either.

However, unless you are living where you were born and you never lived anywhere else, you've probably already done this on a less drastic scale. It's a fact that the population decreases in economically depressed areas as people leave to seek opportunities elsewhere. What they are really doing is *changing their world*, even though they don't think of it in exactly those terms.

In the imaginary scenario, following the imaginary advice drastically alters every single one of the external influences suggested in the list at the beginning of this chapter. Every problem is solved by the action of the individual at the center of his or her world. People actually do pack up and leave their families, but in real life, it seldom ends well, for reasons that will become clear. Besides, this chapter is entitled "Accountability," and that does *not* mean dumping your problems on somebody else or running away from them.

The point of all this is to illustrate to you as clearly as possible that *you* are the #1 influence on what happens in your world. Yes, your spouse has a great deal of influence in your world, but why is your spouse your spouse? Didn't *you* have something to say about that arrangement? And don't you have some contribution toward whatever it is about your spouse that is, shall we say, not optimal? Is it possible a change in your own behavior might help? Furthermore, in the United States, have you ever met a divorced person? What do you think divorce is all about if it's not one or both people changing their world? In the end, like the man said, *"Everybody always* does what they want to do."

The corollary is, "*Everybody doesn't* do what they *don't* want to do."

If you smoke, it's either because you want to smoke or you don't want to quit. It's the same with your job, your relationships, everything. If you are unemployed, it's because you don't want the work that *is* available (and there is *always* work available). If you didn't get a promotion, it's not because of your boss, or your coworkers, or because "life's not fair"; it's because you didn't do what was required to get the promotion. Maybe you were stubborn, or maybe you thought it would be "selling out," but there was certainly something you could have done to get the promotion.

If you stop and think about almost anything that you don't like about your life, you will find there is *something* you can do to make it better. Sometimes, it's pretty drastic, like packing all of your belongings into a U-Haul and moving your family across the country, getting a divorce, or quitting your job. Other times, it might just mean cleaning out the garage, learning a new hobby, or seeing a counselor.

In fact, most of the time *we already know the things we need to do to make things better*, but we don't do them. Again, there are piles of books on positive thinking, books of affirmations, books on building good habits. I'm not going to go into all of that. If you really need hints, you can get all the help you need at the public library. I'm trying to address the root cause, and I believe once you understand the reason your world is the way it is, that understanding will allow you to naturally correct your course.

◆ ◆ ◆

To put it in terms of the concepts we have already introduced, your universe is the sphere from which you get all of your sensory input. As far as you are concerned, like Bomb #20 in chapter 3, you have no indication that anything exists outside your head.

You can take advantage of the technology at your fingertips— or in the case of hitchhiking, at the tip of your thumb—and literally change your entire world in an amazingly short period of time. You don't have to spend a year on a wagon train or weeks on a boat. For about $150 US (in 2014), you can fly just about anywhere in the country. You probably have friends or family all over who would help you restart your life, and you can contact them with the touch of a few buttons.

You can get an online education, you can change jobs, or you can change careers. You can open a basket-weaving business if you like. You can change your habits and behaviors to mend your work environment or your home environment. You can school your children at home. You can join a local theater company or community musical group. If there isn't one where you live, you can start one.

Everything comes down to this: the only person responsible for your world is *you*. The only reason those external influences exist is because *you* tolerate them. The reason you tolerate them is either because *you want* to tolerate them, or *you don't want to do* what it takes to change.

Accountability is when you realize that whatever it is you *think* you want to do, the fact is that your world is the result of what you actually *did* want to do.

Why Do Bad Things Happen to Good People?

That's a truly painful question. I know of a beautiful pair of twin baby girls who have mitochondrial encephalomyopathy. I'm a friend of their grandpa, and until he asked for help in raising funds, I had never heard of the disease. What could they possibly have done (or not) to deserve that disease? How do *those* accounts balance?

Some people would cop out and say it's some kind of payment for something bad they did in another life, or it is some kind of "test" from God. How many times have you heard that "God works in mysterious ways"?

None of those answers work for me, but there is an explanation. There has to be, *because it happened.* What I propose doesn't involve reincarnation or require God to act mysteriously or anything of the sort. That there is an explanation, or a reason, does not make it easy to accept or perhaps even makes it harder. This is a very challenging aspect of this philosophy to accept, and until you think this way for a while, you might not understand the answers.

Recap

- Nature is a far more accurate and factual accountant than I am.

- The vast majority of people want things to add up the way they want, not the way they are.

- Everybody *always* does what they want to do.

- Any person in America has the ability to change his or her entire world by relocating. This is essentially what happens when people move, get a new job, get married or divorced.

- *Accountability* is when you realize that whatever it is you *think* you want to do, your world is the result of what you actually *did*.

7

Awareness
and
Consciousness

Awareness and consciousness are critical concepts, and we'll be spending a bit of time on them. To be *aware* in this context means there is a physical (not intellectual) knowledge of a situation. To be *conscious* is to be aware *and* deliberately responsive to a situation, which implies an intellectual knowledge, no matter how rudimentary.

Pretty much everybody knows plants will grow toward a light source. By definition, then, plants at some level are aware of light, although they have no eyes. On a more basic level, Earth revolves around the sun, so it must be aware of the sun in some way, or it would simply fly off into space. At a higher level, jellyfish move and eat, and some have light receptors (perhaps used to tell up from down), but they have no brain and respond in predetermined ways to specific stimuli, as do plants.

Plants, Earth, and even jellyfish respond to situations, but they do not respond *intentionally*. Therefore, they are not conscious in the way I use the word here. Earth can't say, "Whoa! There's an asteroid coming; I'd better move out of the way!" A plant can't decide *not* to grow toward a light source any more than a jellyfish can make a decision about what to eat; it just tries to digest whatever happens to get caught up in its tentacles.

There are lots of semantic arguments about where consciousness begins. For instance, if you startle a cockroach, it will run *away* from light toward darkness in a very predictable fashion. True, a cockroach running is more complicated than a plant growing, but is the *behavior* really very different than phototropism in plants, which causes movement *toward* light? Consider, then, that the bug might realize that it's running toward a dark baseboard, and based on that new knowledge, alter its course to run under the refrigerator instead. The plant, on the other hand, growing toward a 100-Watt light bulb, will keep doing that until the leaves burn. The difference is the bug can override the predetermined action. The predetermined action can be described as *instinct*, or in the case of a learned behavior—*habit*. For the sake of discussion, let's assume that if a *being* can deliberately alter its instinctive or habitual behavior, it is conscious.

◆ ◆ ◆ ◆

If you pick up a rock and drop it, it will fall toward the center of mass of Earth (to be entirely accurate, Earth also falls toward the rock, but not quite so much). In order for the rock to do that, there has to be some sort of awareness of its situation. "Gravity" is what we call the physical situation for this awareness. Anything with mass is aware of gravity, so it's not such a big deal; I wouldn't put it on your résumé.

There is a tremendous difference between the awareness of a rock and a plant. The plant is aware of gravity; that's a given. However, the rock is pretty much the rock; it was made through a process of natural physical forces and will be eventually altered in the same way. Unless there is some external energy applied, such as pressure or temperature, the rock is not going to change.

The plant, on the other hand, is *alive.* It consumes nutrients and carbon dioxide and emits waste products, and it *reproduces.* Rocks don't make more rocks unless you break them, and even then, you have the same amount of rock, just more pieces. Plants, on the other hand, are composed of tiny little units we call *cells.* They consume gases and solids and convert energy, usually obtained from the sun, into the process of making more cells. The plant grows. It reproduces itself into other plants, and each new plant can be as big as the parent plant. In other words, a plant and its offspring will have greater mass than the original plant. It's strange to think of it, but plants grow in dirt, which is mainly composed of broken-up rocks. In a sense, by absorbing the nutrients from the ground, it means the plant is eating the rocks and turning the basic elements into more plant materials.

This leap from a lifeless rock to a complex photosynthetic plant is pretty huge. You can take a collection of elements in a lab and make a rock. Some of them are *already* rocks, so it's not that tough. All you have to do is build something that sits there and doesn't do anything except fall when you drop it.[1] However, you can't just sit down at a workbench with a bunch of elements and assemble them into a plant. Even with our most advanced science, we have yet to do any more than create parts of a few of the molecules that make up the cell. The magicians who created the

---

[1] This puts me in mind of the Pet Rock. You don't have to feed it and it already knows three tricks: sit, lie down, and stay. I tried teaching mine to fetch, but it would never come back.

mobile phone are not even close to creating something as simple as a single cell, much less an entire plant or animal.

As we move up in complexity to animals, things get very exciting. Take your average household pet—cat, dog, bird, turtle, or whatever you choose. Your pet has a personality. If you have two pets, even the same breed, I'll bet they have distinct personalities. Oh, they might get excited about the same thing, but one will be more outgoing, or one might be dominant. One thing I've noticed about pets—all of them know about food, where to get it, and how. Pets can be very creative about getting food.

That is where *consciousness* (for purposes here) begins—the *deliberate* response to a situation. For instance, my cat will sneak a loaf of bread out of a grocery bag, drag it around the corner, and have a little snack where he thinks nobody can see him (yes, my cat likes bread, but only fresh from the store). Not only did my cat modify his behavior (which is typically sleeping somewhere), he *knew in advance* the whole business about stealing bread would not be received well if he were caught. He scouted the kitchen, waited until nobody was looking, snatched the loot, and got out of sight. You won't see your typical plant doing anything like that!

Your animal, whatever it is, can decide to take a nap. It can decide all on its own it wants to play fetch. It can bark or cry. A turtle can decide to bask in the light or dive in the water. Yes, the behavior can be predictable, but your animal is able to deliberately change its behavior based on the situation and, thus, is not only aware but also conscious.

We know a rock, a plant, an animal, and a person are all aware. There are different levels of awareness between a rock and a plant. The rock reacts only to external physical stimuli, does not grow or change, and does not multiply. The plant does those things, but cannot take deliberate action based on the situation. Animals and people can take deliberate actions. In a forest fire, rocks get hot, trees burn and die. Animals attempt to escape the flames, and people will go even further, either attempting to extinguish or divert the flames to protect other people and their possessions. As the level of consciousness increases, the intentional responses become more sophisticated.

♦ ♦ ♦ ♦

Once, while traveling, I stayed several days at a business-class hotel. I had a late-morning meeting and went down to breakfast after the morning rush. In the hallway, I encountered the housekeeper. Normally, this is not something to write about, but what made this noteworthy was the housekeeper, a young man, was profoundly affected with Down's syndrome. He was obviously mentally handicapped and looking at a door. As I walked up, he pointed at the Do Not Disturb sign and, laying his hands to one side of his head, said, "Asleep. Shhhh."

He then proceeded to push his cart to the next room.

After breakfast, I came back to a nicely cleaned room. Shortly after, a supervisor stopped by to check the room, and I complimented her on the service. I stayed several days at the hotel, and I know there were at least two Down's adults working in housekeeping. It is the only time I can remember writing a note to a hotel manager. I complimented them for providing the opportunity to work for those individuals. They were happy and conscientious workers; you couldn't help but smile every time you saw them because they were always smiling at you (funny how that works). The hotel was a Courtyard by Marriott. I haven't been to that particular hotel in many years, but I sincerely hope they continued the practice.

I bring this up because no matter how clever my cat is, or how brilliantly trained your dog is, or how many words your bird knows, you could *never* teach them the little sign hanging on the door means somebody is asleep inside and not to disturb them and to move on to the next room. Not only that, you could never teach them to clearly communicate the situation to a perfect stranger with two words and a gesture. And I'd really like to see the animal that can be taught to clean a hotel room; I'd be happy with a cat that can clean its own litter box.

You might be a regular genius; you might think you are really intelligent – utterly brilliant – when compared to someone with a mental handicap. But the fact is, when compared to the best and brightest animal, a person with Down's syndrome is your intellectual twin for all intents and purposes. There is *that much difference* between the mind of man and animal.

A Colony of Cells

The human body is a colony of cells. If you cut it into two major parts, the entire colony dies. So, why do we get so upset when somebody dies? What's the big deal? Every time you bake a loaf of bread, or steam fresh vegetables, you kill a colony of cells. If a person is just a colony of cells, then they are no more important than a loaf of bread, right?

We know each person is more than a loaf of bread, more than just a colony of specialized cells. The question is, more *what* than a loaf of bread? *What is it that goes away* when a person dies that makes that particular colony of cells more important than the colonies of cells that make up the food we eat? It must be something, but what is it, where did it come from, and where does it go?

Human Consciousness

I've heard it said that the difference between animal and human consciousness is that an animal cannot conceive of its own death. Perhaps the ability to ask the preceding questions is the difference. What *is* it that makes man different than all other creatures in this world?

The various proposed answers to that question are the root of religions and philosophies through the ages. It is the soul, the consciousness, the universal consciousness, the subconscious, the "*I AM,*" reincarnation, and so many other answers. Here I refer to the consciousness as I've described it—the ability to deliberately respond to a situation of which you are aware.

Just as there are different levels of awareness, there are different levels of consciousness. By this, I most emphatically do *not* mean intelligence. Imagine a situation where you are by far the smartest and most talented thing around. Let's say you are on a boogie board off the Great Barrier Reef in Australia (the "down under") and you have the biggest IQ for miles. You're aware of your surroundings and you are conscious of the waves, especially one that you are planning to pick for a ride. Meantime, in the *really* down under, a Great White Shark is also aware of its surroundings (considering a shark's sensory apparatus, *much* more aware than you) and conscious of a turtle-shaped, dinner-like thing floating on the surface (that would be you).

In this situation, I'm going to bet on the consciousness of the shark over your IQ.

There are a few lessons to be learned from that little tale, the most obvious being that the *situation* has a *lot* to do with results. In fact, as our "situation" (another word for *world*) unfolds, it actually _is_ the result at any given instant. Another lesson is that there are levels of awareness, and levels of consciousness having nothing to do with the size of our brain. What this book is about is *directing your consciousness into desirable situations of your choosing.* We'll be coming back to that theme. What is desirable to the shark is not necessarily desirable to you, but you are in a situation where the consciousness of the shark dominates. And, incidentally, *you* were the genius who paddled your board out there in the first place. Bon Appétit, Monsieur Shark.

◆ ◆ ◆ ◆

For the most part, the consciousness of an animal does not extend deeply into the concept of *time*. Yes, animals have remarkable abilities in terms of timing, but their sense of timing applies only to their immediate situation. My cat did not think in advance, "Hey, I'll bet he's going to the store and I'll bet there will be a loaf of bread in one of those bags. If he puts the bag down to shut the door or something, I'll snag it and run over here to chow down."

No, the cat completely forgot about me while I was gone (it's a good bet he took a nap). Then he heard me come in the door, saw the bread in a bag, saw I wasn't looking, grabbed the bread, and ran. He waited because the other times he grabbed stuff he got yelled at, and he didn't want to be yelled at. So, when I wasn't looking, he grabbed the bread. *After* he got the bread, he didn't want to get yelled at, so he made me vanish by running around the corner. No, the grab-and-go was an impulse response to a situation (as it was for the shark; if it's any consolation, the shark will probably spit you out when it figures out you aren't a turtle).

I, on the other hand, had actually written out a grocery list (on my mobile phone, by the way) because I knew we were low on bread. I also got several other items. Before I got there, the grocer already anticipated that a certain number of people would buy bread today and previously arranged for the baker to supply the bread. The baker knew how much bread he would need even before the grocer, bought the ingredients, and then baked the bread so it would be ready for the order. The flour mill anticipated the order from the baker and ground the flour from the grain already purchased from the farmer, who had harvested the crops from seeds he planted the season before! All in all, it took human beings the better part of a year of advance planning to deliver the loaf of bread to that stupid cat!

That's a lot of advance planning for a simple loaf of bread. It is, however, an example of how people shape the universe around them to obtain a desired result. Once upon a time, somebody somewhere discovered how to make bread. They shared the bread, and people liked it. The problem was there wasn't always grain to make the bread, so somebody got the bright idea of *saving* the grain so they could make bread in the future. Even so, they probably ran out of grain, so the next year they planted more so they could save more. There were obviously far more people who wanted bread than one person could provide, so other people began baking bread to earn their living. The end result, the whole business (busy-ness) of bread making, from storing seeds to your kitchen, was *people* creating a world where bread exists almost everywhere. Some of those people live in a farming world, some in a world of transportation, some in a world of food preparation, while others buy the finished product and sell it to consumers.

If you live in the city, the universe where you live allows you to obtain bread any time of day or night at a supermarket, convenience store, or an all-night diner. However, in order for that to happen, there are people in their universes who are doing the things required to make it possible. *They must exist* in order for you to obtain your bread.

If you live on the farm, your universe is radically different from the city dweller's universe. You may bake your bread, but it's likely you buy it from a store. You have a house, a barn, and equipment to plant and maintain your crops. You probably have some livestock. The city dwellers (and others) purchase the final product from the raw materials you produce, namely the grains. In order for you to maintain your farm and live in your world, *they also must exist*; otherwise, you would have all this grain and nothing to do with it.

Both the city and farm folks enjoy a good movie, and it's one of the few things their universes share in common. They both support the actors and actresses, producers, directors, and supporting personnel in the movie industry, who, in turn, could not exist without their audiences.

♦ ♦ ♦ ♦

I can obviously go on forever describing the complex and intricate ways that we humans have linked our worlds to each other. The closest thing in the animal world is a hive of some sort. However, a child raised on a farm can decide to live in the city after he grows up, and after living there most of his life, move back to the farm. An ant can't just decide it wants to go and live in a beehive for a while and then decide to retire back to the anthill in its old age.

When you *decide* to become a farmer, a lawyer, a politician, a cook, a dishwasher, or whatever, you do so because you are aware of the passage of *time*. You decide to do something in order to change your situation from its current state into something you perceive to be more desirable. You are, with incredible accuracy, *predicting your own future*. I say "with incredible accuracy" because your current situation is the result of everything you have done up to the present moment. Therefore, whatever you are *currently doing* is leading to a specific situation in the future. You are in the process of shaping your future world.

This extended *awareness of time* distinguishes us from other conscious creatures and gives us an enormous advantage over other "aware" or even "conscious" entities. For example, let's think about the future in terms of me and the cat.

The cat learned that when he hears the car, something interesting might happen, so he wakes up and hangs out by the door. He also learned that when he hears grocery bags, it's a lot more likely for something *really* interesting to happen, so he scoots into the kitchen. His ears perk up; he's scouting anything in reach, and, "Hey! Wait a minute! He picked me up and…and…*hey!* He's tossing me in the garage! *What the heck?*"

The preceding is two orders of deliberate response to a situation, with one side order of a future that temporarily does not include a cat in the kitchen.

♦ ♦ ♦ ♦

Talking with my father once, we were discussing how many Italian-Americans would act like their families were such a big deal back in Italy. If that were so, why did they leave? My father was talking about the hard life his parents had after arriving in the USA (they were tailors) and commented that they had left their home and built a new life in an unknown world, all for the sake of their children and grandchildren. Then he said, "It apparently worked."

When I look at my siblings and cousins, I see doctors, nurses, legal assistants, engineers, business owners, musicians, government agents, and the occasional misfit that gives us all something to talk about. There are decorated military heroes, including pilots and commanding officers up to the rank of colonel.

The family has spread from the Atlantic to the Pacific Oceans in all walks of life, because a tailor from Rome and a factory worker from Florence (my two grandfathers) wanted a better life for their descendants. The power of their vision is staggering, yet so few people in the United States realize they are living in a world created for them by their recent ancestors.

Our ability to visualize a future world is responsible for every human achievement. It is why we have schools; it is why we study and why we train our children. It is why we have farmers, bakers, and grocers, as well as doctors, scientists, and engineers.

◆ ◆ ◆ ◆

This ability to visualize a future, and from that vision predict or literally *create* a future, is the subject, either directly or indirectly, of every guide to success. There are tips and techniques; there are exercises to develop good habits that lead to success. There are profound concepts and well-documented knowledge. Some of them are better than others, but pretty much all of them work.

If I had to pick one bit of wisdom, it would be from *Think and Grow Rich*, which states, *"Whatever the mind of man can* ***conceive*** *and* ***believe***, *it can* ***achieve.***"

Look at your world. Do the "Heinlein Daily Miracle" exercise described in chapter 2. Take a good, hard look at your mobile phone. All of those things are the result of people who came up with an idea (concept) and believed it could be done. It is in your world because somebody realized the concept had value they could sell.

Does it need to be miraculous? Not necessarily. I recently bought several bags of dirt and mixed it with some sand to fill in low spots in my yard. We recently planted a tree and bought a few bags of steer manure to give it a good start. I believe the less polite name for "steer manure" is "bullshit." That means there are people out there making an honest living selling sand, dirt, and bullshit, and I'm one of their customers. It's not very miraculous, but it's certainly pretty amazing when you think about it.

Recap

- To be "conscious" is to be *aware and deliberately responsive* to a situation.

- The level of consciousness of any person, even one of low intelligence, is profoundly greater than even the best and brightest animal.

- This book is about *directing your consciousness into desirable situations of your choosing.*

- People shape the universe around them to obtain a desired result and have been doing so since society began.

- When you do something to change your situation into something more desirable, you are, with incredible accuracy, predicting your own future.

- Your current actions are leading to a specific situation in the future. *You are in the process of shaping your world.*

- The ability to visualize a future world is responsible for every human achievement.

- This ability to visualize a future, and from that vision predict or literally *create* a future, is the subject, either directly or indirectly, of every guide to success, and pretty much all of them work.

8

Crafting Spells

You've learned that miracles surround you every day and that you should pay attention to these miracles because they enable you to envision an even more miraculous future. We established that your understanding of the entire universe is the result of information you obtain through your senses; therefore, you are effectively the center of your universe, and you take it with you wherever you go. You also know that most of our technology works like magic as far as you are concerned. You can communicate at will using invisible rays and invisible engravings and mysterious energy sources. Hopefully, you also know that you really don't know very much at all about this technology, so it *might as well* be magic. You know that nature is a meticulous and incorruptible accountant, and now realize that *you* are the single biggest determining factor in your universe, whether you want to admit it or not. We have discussed awareness and consciousness and described different levels of both.

That's quite a tour! Now, we get to the "how to" part. I've mentioned a few times that using success principles yields results that seem like magic. Because success principles are available to anybody, that makes our world a lot like the imaginary world where everybody has magical talent but few actually believe in magic. These next couple of chapters are your personal Hogwarts, where you will learn to use your natural-born talent for shaping your world. I figured if the results are like magic, I might as well call using success principles "magic spells." It's not magic, by the way, it just seems like it. The concepts are actually pretty simple, and you will most likely be familiar with many of them.

This reminds me of a successful weight loss program I participated in. You may recall from my "Personal Journey" in the preface that I was fat. I like to think I'm more knowledgeable than the average person when it comes to nutrition, but like so many Americans, I was getting nowhere with regard to losing weight. Well, one day, I was walking to my car after an errand and dropped my keys. I looked up, and I was standing in front of Quick Weight Loss Centers of Atlanta. By now, I fully realized that when there is something you want to achieve, opportunities will sometimes just smack you right in the face; the trick is to recognize them when they happen. This seemed to be one of those times, so I walked in the door.[1]

The fact is that the weight loss program didn't tell me anything new. My first comment when my wife asked me about it was, "I think my first-grade teacher told me that stuff."

I lost thirty pounds in the first two months, and went on to lose ten more. That was six years ago, and I have not only maintained my weight, I actually weigh less now than when I finished the program.

As far as weight loss goes, it's not a matter of going "on a diet." Everybody is "on a diet." Diet simply refers to what you eat

---

[1] Once, I was thinking of moving to a new state, and a tanker truck drove off a bridge and exploded in front of my rental car as I was going to look at real estate. I took that hint, too, and decided not to move.

and drink. If you want to change your weight (more accurately, your health), you need to change what you eat and drink; that is, your diet. There's no big trick to it; you can probably make a list of good and bad foods. However, there are some very specific habits (good and bad) that make a tremendous difference in your weight and health.

You are already eating. All you need to do is change what *you are eating to get different results.*

Success principles are very much like maintaining a healthy weight. In terms of success principles:

You are already doing the things that will lead to your future. If you don't like (or don't know) where you are currently headed, you need to do different things.

In terms of body weight, you're already eating. In terms of success, you're already doing. If you don't like your weight, you need to change what you're eating. If you don't like your results, you need to change what you're doing.

♦ ♦ ♦ ♦

This chapter deals with the practical application of fundamental principles. When we use them intentionally (consciously) to achieve a specific result, we call them success principles. These fundamental principles work for both success *and* failure. You are using them every day of your life. There is no success or failure in science; there are only actions and results. The universe doesn't care whether you succeed or fail any more than your car cares whether or not you get to work on time. Fortunately, we figured out the behaviors that we call success principles increase your chances of success. The scientific explanations of these principles come later in the book. This chapter is about how to *use* them.

♦ ♦ ♦ ♦

Remember my Wise Fraud from the preface? He had a seminar entitled, "How to Make $100,000 a Year." It was very well attended. This was back in the early 1980s, when $100,000 was a *lot* of money. The first two words out of his mouth were, "Sell junk."

He then told us we now knew everything we needed to know to make $100,000 per year and he could leave, except that we would probably all feel cheated (he was right about that!). He then explained that no self-respecting junk dealer ever made less than $100,000 per year. He was dead serious and proceeded to teach us how to sell junk! The scary part is that the business of successfully selling junk applies to a whole lot of things. Shortly after the seminar, I applied the principles he taught, ended up quitting my job, and in less than six months, *quintupled* my salary. And I was *not* selling junk, by the way, so don't just quit your job and start living at flea markets without knowing what you are doing. I applied the *principles* to my knowledge of engineering and computers, and I ended up making a little over $100,000 that year (what a coincidence).

The reason I mention this is that if I had to describe the most important thing that turns a fundamental principle (what we do every day) into a *Success Principle,* it would be this: **"Write it down."**

If all I said was *"write it down,"* I'd be doing the same thing to you as our Wise Fraud did to me, except a book is a *lot* cheaper than that three-day seminar, and you get three words and I only got two. So, like my fraudulent mentor, from whom you would gladly buy a bottle of snake oil (it would probably work!), I'll fill you in on the details, such as what you need to write down, and how it all works.

♦ ♦ ♦ ♦

The title of this chapter is "Crafting Spells." This is where you learn the ingredients that make up a good spell.

By the way, please understand that when I refer to a spell, I'm referring to *technology indistinguishable from magic.* I am *not* suggesting you are practicing any occult rituals, or that there is anything suggestive of any kind of religion or mysticism. I have neither intent nor desire to comment on God or religion. It is a matter of faith, and your faith is a personal matter. Nothing I'm suggesting in this book conflicts with any faith that I know, any more than believing that Earth is round like a ball is a conflict.

So, no, you aren't doing magic. You're really just setting goals. It just happens to work like magic. You have to admit, though, that casting spells sounds a lot more fun than setting goals.

Sonett Story

I believe I was about nineteen or twenty years old the first time I consciously employed success principles. I was reading the book *Think and Grow Rich* and followed the directions in the chapter on "Autosuggestion." I was particularly interested in hypnosis and autosuggestion and had previously learned quite a bit about these topics. I was young and stupid, so given the opportunity to achieve anything in the world, I decided on a sports car.

I wrote down a statement of what I wanted—an orange Saab Sonett III with black racing stripes and psychedelic, soccer ball wheels. I described it in detail and added some unintended modifications of my own (the stripes were different, the wheels and interior were not available for that car, engine modifications were not available, and a few other items).

I got creative with the instructions from the book and wrote the statement on 3 x 5 index cards. I read a lot, so I used the cards as bookmarks. Shortly, I forgot all about the statement (how many times can you read a bookmark?) and the goal of getting the car. Eventually, the books ended up on the shelf with the cards still inside. A few years later, I opened a book for some reason and found the forgotten statement on the card inside the book.

The car, exactly as I had described it, complete with my custom modifications, was sitting in my driveway. Obviously, the experiment worked. It also scared the crap out of me, and it was a long time before I messed around success principles again.

♦ ♦ ♦ ♦

"Big fat deal," you say, "what's the mystery?"

The obvious explanation is that I wanted the car before I wrote the statement. Afterward, I still wanted the car and ended up buying it, right? Wrong. Part of the mystery was that I could not afford that car, even a used one. Then one day, I bought a wrecked Sonett from a friend. It was $1,000, and I used to joke about paying $1 per piece; the front of the car was a total loss. Then one day, I saw another wrecked Sonett on the back of a tow truck. This car had slid backward off the road into a tree; the front was in perfect shape, but the rear of the car was destroyed. I followed the tow truck and bought the wreck on the spot from the driver for three hundred dollars and had him tow it to my house.

Now I had all of the parts needed in order to make a car. I fixed or replaced the broken items and then literally bolted and welded the two cars together at the engine firewall. While I was assembling these two cars into one, I made certain "improvements," never once thinking about the statement hidden away in the book. My total cost was a fraction of the value of the finished car. The biggest expense was the material I used for the blue and gray upholstery (one of the several modifications not available from the dealer).

Why was that so frightening? When I saw the card in the book, *it was as though all of the intervening time between writing the statement and owning the car simply vanished.* It felt like the car just went *poof* and appeared in my driveway just as I had described it years before.

♦ ♦ ♦ ♦

Suppose somebody tells you that if you want a particular member of the opposite sex to be attracted to you, all you have to do is cross your fingers and whisper "abracadabra." Of course, you wouldn't believe it. Later on, you happen to see somebody attractive, and just for the heck of it, you cross your fingers and whisper "abracadabra." Suddenly, the person turns around, sees you, and comes over and tries to pick you up.

You would *not* think, "Gee, how cool!"

It would make you very uncomfortable. At best, you might think it was just your natural animal magnetism and a total coincidence (except if you had such animal magnetism, you wouldn't be muttering "abracadabra" under your breath and hoping for a miracle). At worst, you might just bolt out the door, find a priest, and confess. If it happened again and you established a relationship, you would never trust whether the person actually liked *you* or was compelled to like you by some unknown force. You would probably wonder if the "abracadabra" would wear off and leave the poor person with a really bad case of morning-after regret.

That is the natural human reaction to anything we don't understand. In fact, distrust or outright fear of the unknown is a survival trait of the entire animal kingdom. Even the most fearsome predators will keep their distance until they have a chance to assess a new situation. You and I are no different.

That's the way it was for me. It was obvious that whatever I did worked, but not knowing exactly how it happened (or worse, I *did* know exactly what happened, but didn't know *why*) made me feel distinctly uncomfortable.

The result was that I was reluctant to try this success stuff again. It was as though I didn't know how many magic bullets I had in this gun, and I wanted to make sure I used them on really important stuff. Later, when something really important *did* come up, I wouldn't try it just in case it *didn't* work (so much for logical thinking). What I didn't realize was that I was doing these things *all of the time anyway* (and so are *you*).

We'll revisit this concept in more detail later. This is the "how to" chapter, and by "how to," I really mean "how-to-*on-purpose.*" After reading the rest of the book, you will come to understand that you are already doing these things and that success principles are just a matter of doing the *right* things, very similar to eating the *right* foods instead of eating the *easiest* foods.

The goal is that you obtain the results you want, and the understanding you gain from this book will make your experience more *dra*matic and less *trau*matic.

♦ ♦ ♦ ♦

I closed the previous chapter with the concept from Napoleon Hill: *Whatever the mind of man can conceive and believe, it can achieve.* This concept is at the core of the "how to."

The idea is to think of something and then believe it can be done. For instance, the mobile phone could not be invented in the nineteenth century. Although it was possible to conceive of the idea of communicating across vast distances (remember the magic candles?), there was no context in the physical world to support the creation of such a portable device. There was no telephone infrastructure; there were no GPS satellites (the Wright brothers hadn't even got off the ground, yet); and no lithium batteries. Even though people could imagine the *result* (talking across long distances), there was no possible way to imagine the workings of the actual *device*.

However, once electricity, the telephone, radio, space travel, and all of the other separate technologies were achieved, it became possible to imagine the marriage of these separate technologies. Soon after that, somebody actually built the mobile phone and the infrastructure to support it. That poses an interesting question: did we invent the mobile phone because we invented all of the other things, or did we invent all of the other things so we could invent the mobile phone? What magical technology is going to be built upon the already amazing mobile phone? I don't know, but I can say that it will be something that could not be imagined until we held the mobile phone in our hands.

You are in the process of creating your future right now, whether you know it or not. Everybody everywhere is doing the same thing for *their* future, whether *they* know it or not. The part that screws everybody up is "whether they know it or not." Most people don't know it. What *you* will be doing is *knowing* as opposed to not knowing. *You* will be *knowingly* creating your future.

Crafting the Spell

It all comes down to the visualization of what you want to happen—and the belief it *can* happen. This is Hogwarts, and in this class we're learning to craft a spell. We'll be casting our magic fishhook into the universe and we're going to reel something in. When we do, we'd like it to be something pleasant. Surprises are fine for special occasions, but for advance planning, we want things to unfold as we expect. We ensure this by following three simple steps:

1. Create the complete picture of what you want.
2. Figure out when it's going to happen.
3. Write it down.

That's pretty much it. Sounds simple, but there's more to it than you might think! Let's break each step down in detail.

Step 1: Create the Complete Picture of What You Want

This is by far the most complicated of the three steps. A subtitle for this topic might be, *"Be careful what you wish for; you just might get it."*

For instance, when I was a child, I wanted to be an airplane pilot and fly for a living when I grew up. Well, I have a pilot's license, but I also have a million frequent flyer miles. I used to joke that flying in the middle seat in the back of the plane wasn't what I had in mind when I said I wanted to fly. I realize now that it's not very funny. The desire I had as a child was unfocused and incomplete, and that lack of focus is reflected in my world. I got what I wanted, but not what I *really* wanted.

There are three things you need to define in order to complete your picture:

a) What you want.
b) What you are giving up in order to get what you want.
c) Your world after you get what you want.

They are all very important, so I will cover them in detail.

Step 1a: Picture What You Want

I get more questions about this part of the process than anything else. Most Americans are simply not taught to do this. I mentioned in chapter 1 that getting a job has become the de facto goal of the American middle class. Once you get a job, your next goal is to either get a promotion or get a better-paying job. In other words, after getting a job, the goal becomes "get another job."

It's pretty surprising what happens when you ask people what they want their future to be. Most people really don't give it any thought at all, which goes a long way toward explaining why people end up living lives entirely different than they expected. They expect nothing in particular, and that's exactly what they get.

If you really have no idea what you want out of life, you probably need to start small. This process *does* work for big things like your wealth, your health, relationships, as well as material things, but you might be in a situation where it's not even possible to imagine, much less believe, that you can achieve those things. Remember the mobile phone; it couldn't be invented until other technologies were in place.

So, don't overlook the small things in life. They are very important. There are entire books out there on how to *Think Big*, and I absolutely agree that you should have a grand vision of your future. That's part of thinking things through. On the other hand, it's just as important to mow the lawn, wash the car, or get your license renewed.

It is easier to achieve individual tasks instead of broad categories. Instead of "I wanna be rich," focus instead on individual tasks, such as paying off your credit cards and becoming debt-free. Meantime, you can also focus on getting your house and belongings in order and perhaps, too, your health, relationships, and occupation. Once you feel good, your relationships are the way you want them, your house is in top shape, and you've cleaned up your credit situation, you will have a lot more options. You will get to the point where things you could not believe were possible are now within reach. All of those smaller achievements are steps on the way toward the rich world you want to live in.

Step 1b: Picture What Are You Going to Give Up

Once you figure out what you want, figure out what you are going to give up in order to get what you want. *There Ain't No Such Thing As A Free Lunch (TANSTAAFL);* I mentioned that earlier in the book, and here's where we return to the subject. I think of it as a different way of stating the first law of thermodynamics, or the conservation of energy.[2]

> *"When you get something for nothing, you just haven't been billed for it yet."* – **Chinese Fortune Cookie**[3]

Understanding that in order to get something, you need to give up something is a critical concept. If you don't understand this,

---

[2] The law of conservation of energy states that the total energy of an isolated system is constant; energy can be transformed from one form to another, but cannot be created or destroyed.

[3] I actually got that fortune cookie while writing this chapter!

nothing is ever going to work out quite the way you want. This is not optional; there is always a price to pay.

- *You want a Ferrari*: Do you know how much one of those things costs to own and maintain?

- *You want a successful business*: Do you know how much work and responsibility that requires?

Be *absolutely clear what you are going to do or pay or give up* to obtain what you desire. Dedicating your time to munching snacks while sitting on the couch watching TV is not going to get you much of anything, unless your goal is to become mentally and physically out of shape. "What if I want to make a lot of money by munching snacks while sitting on the couch watching TV?" you ask.

Are you prepared to live a life that consists solely of sitting on a couch and eating junk food? What kind of legacy is that? What about your health? Are you *really* willing to do that? Author Gene Wolfe wrote the beautiful short story *Kevin Malone* that deals with the concept of "free" wealth. Hunt it down and read it.

Are you willing to give up TV? Are you willing to work harder? Are you willing to do some research? Are you willing to give up cheesecake? Are you willing to lose your neighborhood friends and change your kid's school to get a better home? Are you willing to go to school yourself if that's required for the life you desire? You can be a top surgeon if you want, but there's a lot of hard work and effort between where you are now and being a top surgeon. The same is true for an airline pilot, lawyer, CEO, or business owner. Are you willing to risk quitting your job? That may be what it takes to achieve what you want.

Then there's the whole business of our *poor-but-fulfilled* culture. We have been taught in many subtle and not-so-subtle ways people and businesses get rich by taking advantage of other people in some immoral or illegal fashion. You probably already think it's morally *wrong* to get too far ahead in this world, and you need to overcome that nonsense. This kind of thinking crossed my mind when I thought about my Saab Sonett. Did I make those two people wreck their cars?

No, all *I* did was be at the right place at the right time. *They* were the ones who wrecked their cars, and you and I both know who the #1 influence in *their* worlds was—it was them. I paid for *my* car with money, time, and labor. It wasn't free.

That's another reason to spell out what *you* are going to give up in order to obtain what you desire. That way you *know* you are footing the bill, and unfounded feelings of guilt are not going to become a self-imposed obstacle. Whatever it is you receive, it is always paid in advance.

You can't get a house and build it later. It has to be built *before* you can live in it, plain and simple. I spent a year of nights and weekends working in the garage before I was able to drive my Sonett. Even before buying our loaf of bread, the first person to pay was the farmer long before it came into my possession. From seed to my kitchen, it was paid for by somebody every step of the way.

Another bit of wisdom from the Wise Fraud was about wealth. He asked, "A lot of people want to be wealthy, but don't understand what wealth is. How do you get wealth?"

After we gave him a bunch of wrong answers ranging from selling junk to robbing banks, he answered, "You *buy* it."

Well, duh. He went on to explain that money wasn't wealth. An accumulation of valuable *things* was wealth, and you get *things* by buying them. Anybody who has money without wealth is called a miser, and who wants to be a miser?

It's the same principle here—whatever it is you achieve must be paid for. The good news is that your payment does not need to be unpleasant, nor does it need to burden your life. Where the payment comes from is very flexible. It might be your time. It might be unrelated to the situation. It might even seem to be inadequate payment.

For instance, you can buy a car you want by selling the car you currently *don't* want as well as a lot of stuff you also don't want or need. Perhaps you can finance a new car for the same payment you currently have on your existing car. You can clean out the garage, get your life in order, have a new set of wheels, and be in exactly the same or better financial situation. You can unburden your life on the way to creating the world you want to live in.

Recently, I wanted a car I could not afford. I had a job with a specific bonus structure. I figured that in order for me to get the car, my team would need to sell an additional $2M in the next four quarters above and beyond our past performance in order for me to earn a sufficient bonus to make the purchase. That was a significant amount of additional sales, but it had been done before. I calculated that it would take fifteen months—twelve months earning and three months from ordering the car to taking delivery. I wrote fifteen months down as the time frame, and I was going to do everything in my power to make an extra $2M for the team in the coming twelve months. I got the car seven months early; we closed a huge sale and I had an unexpected change in my personal finances. I had the money, and then some guy who had ordered one of these cars backed out of his purchase. I negotiated an excellent price with the dealer to take the car off his hands, and drove it off the lot three days later, instead of three months.

A musician I know bought a good guitar for a good price, and kept buying, selling, and trading guitars, always increasing the quality, until he had a vintage Gibson Les Paul that was exactly what he wanted, worth thousands of dollars. Having made a little bit of money on each transaction, by the time he got the Les Paul, he had all of the money he paid for the first guitar in his pocket, *plus* a couple of extra guitars for trading purposes in case another good opportunity came along.

Then there is the story of Kyle McDonald, who started bartering with a single red paperclip, until he had traded up to owning a house in a year and a day.[4]

You can specify your time, your effort, a promotion, a new job, an additional source of income, a new opportunity, cleaning out your garage on eBay, mowing lawns on the side for extra money, just about anything you can conceive of that will move you toward your goal. If you want a loving, caring, and understanding mate, you can pay for that by *you* fulfilling the needs of your mate (even if you think you already are).

Step 1c: Picture Your World Like after this Happens

You will get consistent results if you can *clearly picture* what you want and can hold that image in your mind. Visualize driving your dream automobile; visualize looking good in that swimsuit; visualize a happy relationship. What does it mean to your daily life? How does it affect your self-confidence? If you lose weight,

---

[4] http://www.oneredpaperclip.com

your clothes fit better, you are healthier, your knees won't hurt, and there will be a spring in your step. Imagine choosing among several swimsuits based on how good you make *them* look, instead of how much fat they hide.

When looking for a desired *result*, it's very important to *think through the entire process.* Instead of learning to fly an airplane, consider learning to *land* an airplane instead, which is actually a lot more difficult and far more important. Whether you want a car, a home, a career, or a pile of money, it doesn't matter. You must be able to clearly visualize the entire result you want; not just getting something, but what happens after you get it.

Think of the stories you have heard of the genie that grants three wishes. So often, the wishes end badly because the person making the wishes has not thought things through. It is more important to create a picture of the *result* that you desire than to picture the thing itself.

You also need to put yourself in the picture. Have you ever suddenly realized somebody was talking to you and you hadn't heard a word that was said? That's probably because the person didn't say your name first. Have you noticed that when you say, "Excuse me, sir (or ma'am)," it doesn't always work? You usually have to say it again. If you just start talking without addressing anybody in particular, then nobody in particular is going to pay attention. You can yell, "Hey, *you!*" to get somebody's attention, but saying the person's name will be much more effective.

The same is true for *you.* You are trying to get your own attention, or more precisely, the attention of your consciousness. You are the center of your universe. You are also the #1 factor in determining what happens in your universe. If you just write down

"I wanna," then your consciousness might just think, "Yeah, you and everybody else."[5]

When you specify what is going to happen in your world, you need to put yourself directly in the picture. You need to say, "*This* is exactly what's going to happen to *me*, this is *when* it's going to happen, and this is *how* it's going to happen."

Step #2: Figure Out When It's Going to Happen

Step #1 is creating the complete picture of what you want. As we get into the science behind the success principles, you will see that the process we're discussing is actually describing a place—a place where you have achieved what you desire. Setting a time is simply another part of describing that place.

Think about the riddle, *"How can two automobiles occupy the same parking space?"* Answer: the second car can use the space after the first car leaves.

Or, suppose you're meeting somebody for coffee. You both agree that it will be the coffee shop on Main Street. What's missing? You haven't set a time. If you don't set a time, the meeting is not going to happen. Once you set a time, say Thursday at 2 p.m. at the coffee shop on Main Street, then you have fixed the meeting location in space and time. The reason time is required to describe any kind of event is because time is actually a measurement used to describe the physical location of a particular event.

Let's say you want to own a house, but you don't specify when you want it. It might show up in your world thirty years later than you wanted. Bummer. I heard of a fellow who wanted a

---

[5] This is *your* consciousness. Wouldn't you say that?

Cadillac in his driveway. A couple of years after going bankrupt and losing his home, he drove by the place, and there in the driveway was a new Cadillac.

"*I wanna be rich someday*" is as foolish a goal as "*I wanna be rich tomorrow.*" Either one might happen, but the odds are stacked against you pretty badly. Pick a time frame you can believe. Say you want to become debt-free. You'd be surprised how fast that can happen if you focus on that instead of focusing on buying toys and eating out. Get a calculator and figure it out. Go to a debt counselor.

In the preface, I shared my personal story, and earlier in this chapter I mentioned wanting a new car. It was just over three years from not having a car, not having an income, and being buried in debt until I was able to buy the car of my dreams. Three years sounds like a long time, but if you think back three years in your life, it wasn't that long ago.

In fact, recall that when I sat down and wrote out my future, I didn't start with some big fancy car. I just needed a car. I ended up with a twenty year old Chevy Celebrity with a busted window. At the time, any car that got me from Point A to Point B qualified as the car of my dreams. After I got the Chevy, I established an income and was able to advance that income to the point where I could think about a new car. Just *one* of the tires on my new car is worth more than the entire Chevy, but that Chevy did its job.

I am *not* telling you only to set goals that are easily attained. I *am* telling you there is such a thing as inertia in this Universe, and if you've been eating yourself fat and spending yourself poor, you are not going to be skinny and rich next week. If you are dead in the water, it's going to take a little bit of time to get moving again.

When you are setting your time frame, be aggressive but don't make it impossible. As you gain experience and confidence, you will find things will happen more and more quickly.

Step #3: Write It Down

I mentioned earlier *writing down your goals is the single thing that will have the most impact on your success.* If you have read any book on how to succeed, it tells you to write down your goals, but the fact is that very few people actually follow up on that simple item, and that is probably the single biggest reason people do not achieve the success they expect.

It reminds me of weight loss plans. Any plan worth the paper it's printed on tells the reader to drink a certain amount of water, and by a certain amount, I mean a couple of quarts more than what most Americans normally drink. I think most people on a weight loss plan fail to drink enough water, usually justifying their actions by saying that diet soda, coffee, and iced tea count. I know I used the all those excuses. It wasn't till after I lost a lot of weight that I realized the importance of plain old water. I lost another fifteen pounds after I started drinking enough water, *without* changing my diet. So here's two hints:

1. If you want to lose weight, pay attention to the bit about drinking water, and don't cheat.
2. If you want to be a success, pay attention to the bit about writing things down, and don't cheat.

With rare exceptions, everything created by man is first written down. Music is written. Buildings are drawn, sketched, and designed. There are thousands of drawings that go into the manufacture of your mobile phone. The shows you see on television are scripted. Even the comedians at the Improv write their comic material down and practice it. *Everything* is written down somewhere. Art is the written visions of artists, and even then they often sketch what they want to create. Somebody wrote down the plans to build the bag to package steer manure. For crying out loud, you are trying to change your *world*—don't you think it merits the same care used to package manure?

A lot of books address this subject. They deal with concepts such as autosuggestion, establishing lines of communication between your conscious and subconscious minds, the manifestation of an insubstantial pattern of thought into a physical manifestation, and other ideas. It's actually not that complicated; it's just a matter of remembering what you think.

Your consciousness is dealing with the sensory input from the entire universe all of the time. There are miracles happening all around you that you really don't understand, and suddenly you think of something, maybe something important. Later on, the only thing you can remember is that you were excited because you thought of something, *but you can't remember what it was.* If you don't write it down, you are probably going to forget it. It's like trying to remember a dream. The only way to remember a dream is to keep a pen and paper by your bed and write it down immediately. If you get up to walk downstairs to get a pen, you will forget the dream. Contrary to popular wisdom, your thoughts are *not* things; your thoughts are no more than dreams.

Inside your brain, there is no touch, smell, taste, sight, or sound apparatus. When you think of something, all you have is a pattern of neurons firing in the frontal lobe of your cerebral cortex. There's no really good internal mechanism to get that pattern from there to the part of your brain used for long-term memory. You need to *take the thought out of your head*, put it on a piece of paper, to *put it back in your head.* When you write the thought down, you are using your touch and sight as sensory input. Your senses *are* connected to the part of the brain that is built to remember. The thought that originated in one part of your brain is now being stored in a different part, and *the part where it is stored is the part that remembers!*

You may say all day long that *thoughts are things* and *dreams are powerful,* but if you do not write them down, the noise from living in your daily world is going to dilute and alter your thoughts or erase them entirely. The act of writing something down *forces* your consciousness to focus and then commits it to memory. It has now become sensory input, and sensory input is something your brain remembers very well.

Got that?

I'll give you an example of taking something out of your head and putting it into physical form to get your own attention. I misplaced my keys while visiting my father in his later years of life. He said,

> "I used to do that. I thought I was getting dementia. One day, I was working in the garage using a hammer. I reached for the hammer, and it was *gone.*
>
> "I looked all over for that damned hammer, and I was getting more and more pissed off. It's not a big garage, and I had just been using the hammer, and what the *hell* did I do with it? I thought I'd finally killed my last useful brain cell and just gave up, went and got a glass of wine to calm down, and sat down in the living room to watch TV.
>
> "There was the hammer, sitting on the end table right next to the phone. Well, how in the *hell* the hammer got to the

living room was about to drive me crazy when I realized Joanne called for your mother and wanted me to leave her a message.

"I didn't *forget* where I put the hammer; *I never even knew I put the hammer down!* I just answered the phone with the hammer in my hand and put it down to pick up the pen. I was listening to Joanne talk and was thinking about the pen, *not the hammer.*

"So, after that, whenever I put something down, I say out loud, *'I just put the hammer on the end table.'*

"Now I don't forget things like that. I cured my dementia!"

My father was a bright guy, but it took him most of his life to figure out that little trick, which is better than a lot of people who are still misplacing their hammers. I'll bet you've done the same thing. You're focused on something, and you put your keychain (wallet, glasses, purse, etc.) in some odd place, and then you can't find it even though you know you had it two minutes earlier. We once found our missing phone in the refrigerator (no, I'm not the one who put it there).

When you say, "I put the phone in the refrigerator" *out loud*, you focus your attention, then you hear the words with your ears (sensory input) and will now remember where you put the phone (purse, keys, wallet, or whatever). Try it; you'll be amazed.[6]

---

[6] Somebody asked, "If you don't notice that you're doing something, how can you remember to say it out loud?" It actually is a habit you can develop, just like intentionally saying somebody's name out loud after you meet them. Just start telling yourself *every time* you put something down.

You might already know that writing something down in the form of taking notes helps you remember the topic, or saying a person's name out loud helps you to remember the name. That's just the start. When you reread your notes, or talk to or about the person using the person's name, it reinforces what you wrote or said. You are *directing your consciousness*, a subject we will review in more detail.

Writing your goal down places it in your conscious memory. If you don't write it down, it is not in your memory and not available to your consciousness. You want to write down the complete picture as described earlier—exactly what you want, what you are giving up, and how it will change your world. Finally, write down the when you expect this to happen.

Recap

- These aren't really magic spells! It's science!

- The composition of a "spell" is:

  1. Create the *complete* picture of what you want.
  2. Figure out when it's going to happen.
  3. Write it down.

- The <u>complete</u> picture includes:

  a) What you want.
  b) What you are giving up in order to get what you want.
  c) Your world after you get what you want.

- You are writing things down to get the thought out of the thinking part of your brain and into the remembering part of your brain – your conscious memory.

9

Casting Spells

In the last chapter you learned what goes into a good spell: you need to *write down* a *complete picture* of what you want, including *when you expect it to happen*.

This chapter deals with the practical application of those essential tasks, and also what to do now that you have all the pieces in place. Remember, there is no success or failure; there are only actions and results. This chapter is about actions.

The title of this chapter is "Casting Spells." There are several definitions of the word *cast*, but I especially like two of them: one involves throwing a baited hook into the water, and the other involves a procedure that causes a magical spell to take effect. In a sense, when you do what I suggest, you are casting a spell that will cause your universe to change before your very eyes, and in another sense, you're fishing. I'm telling you how to (metaphorically) catch fish.

Once again, please understand that when I say we are casting a spell, I'm referring to *technology indistinguishable from magic,* not any sort of occult ritual or mysticism. This is all about creating and achieving goals in a very practical manner.

Casting the Spell

This is the part where we actually cast our magic fishhook into the universe to reel something in. In the last chapter you learned to:

1. Create the complete picture of what you want.
2. Figure out when it's going to happen.
3. Write it down.

That last item, the written spell, is the main focus of this chapter. Later in the chapter you will see some specific examples that you can use to craft your own spells, but first I'd like to mention a few things.

Use a Piece of Paper

Getting back to stereotypes, you would probably think that an engineer and technology consultant would be somewhat of a gadget nerd, and in my case you would be entirely correct. I once had a sixteen-channel sound board attached to my computer, but that was only because my twelve-channel board was in the shop. What? You don't have both a twelve- and a sixteen-channel mixer? How do you connect your computer, tablets and other toys into your four-channel recorder and stereo sound system?

Yes, I love technology, and I have perhaps just a few more toys than I actually need. So, believe me when I tell you that I have yet to find any electronic media that works as well as writing your spell out on a plain old piece of paper. I won't go so far as to suggest you use a goose quill pen on parchment; a Bic pen on notebook paper will work just fine.

There are wonderful applications on fantastic devices available. In the case of touch-screen tablets, now available for iOS, Android, and Windows, there are applications that actually let you write notes in your own hand using a stylus. Those are wonderful applications, and I've been using them to take notes since the first iPad came out. In fact, that ancient iPad is here at my desk plugged into the aforementioned mixer. I have graduated to newer technology for note-taking by hand. However, although technology is great for taking notes, it does *not* work as well for casting spells.

Back in the previous century, when men were men, and women were men, too, and there was no such thing as a child-proof cap on the bottle of aspirin, and children were allowed, no, *encouraged* to stop bothering everybody and run free in the neighborhood, engineers used to draw things on paper (called *vellum*). The vellum was gradually replaced by a new miracle of technology called Mylar, a coated polyester film. That's when I started my design career, in the late 1960s. Yes, engineers used to actually draw stuff with pen and pencil. Then came the computer revolution in the 1980s, and it became economically viable to migrate from pencil-on-Mylar to Computer Aided Design and Drafting (CADD). That is when I transitioned from brick-and-mortar engineer to technology consultant. I had a talent for the computer stuff.

I noticed something very quickly; I became very easily distracted using the computer compared to using a drawing board. Even before I launched my consulting career, I figured out what was happening. In fact, this understanding actually was one of the reasons for the success I enjoyed as a consultant.

When working on drawings (often as large as 34" x 44"), I could set my pencil down, go home, party all weekend, recover on Sunday, and come back to work on Monday morning. I'd sit down at my desk, pick up my pencil, and be back up to speed in just a minute.

Working on the computer, I'd get on a phone call for just a couple of minutes, but it would take me five or ten minutes to figure out what I was doing before the call, even though I never got out of my chair.

Here's what was going on. With a drawing, the whole thing was laid out right in front of me. I could take in the entire design with just a glance. Figuring out where to start was just a matter of finding the missing parts, which was usually pretty obvious because that was usually where I left my pencil.

On the computer, after a few minutes, the screen would go dark and had to be lit up again. I might still be working on a 34" x 44" drawing, but the screen could be anything from a 14" (diagonal) screen to, at most, a 19" screen.[1] I could only see a piece of the drawing. If I zoomed out to see the whole thing, it was too small to read anything useful. If the session picked up in the same zoomed-in view, I couldn't see parts of the drawing that were essential to the view I was working on. I'd need to zoom out in stages till I got enough of the overall picture for my mind to click in to what I had been doing before the interruption.

I am not a technophobe. In fact, I'm what marketing folks call an "early adopter." I'm using the latest hardware and software to write this book (not to mention multiple 32" screens!). I have three touch-screen devices, and I carry my stylus to take notes on one of my tablets, where they are organized and synchronized in the cloud. I've worked with some of the largest corporations in the world, as well as several governments, on their technical infrastructure. When I'm not writing or consulting, I'm playing

---

[1] In the 1980's, a 19" graphics monitor cost over $20,000!

music somewhere. Even then, I use the latest technology to keep sheet music for thousands of songs available with a few touches.

I have tried all of the technical tricks. In fact, I *want* to be able to use technology for this. I can save you a lot of time and just tell you – don't even try. It's just like CADD vs. Mylar, except when you are casting spells, you don't have the luxury of hunting around for where you left off. The whole *point* is to keep it right at the front of your conscious mind, and there just isn't anything like plain old-fashioned paper to do that. Even with the advanced CADD systems of today, ultimately they still print out those 34" x 44" drawings when it's time to go build something.

Remember that the intention here is to fix your goal in your memory so your consciousness can access that memory. The reason for addressing your consciousness is detailed later in the book.

What happens when you use an electronic device for casting your spells is that you can see only one thing at a time when you use the device. By default, you miss out on the big picture.

The way we learn our goals is the way we learn most things— through repetition. There are other ways to learn, but repetition is what applies here. Writing it down is the first step. If you don't write it down, it's just a figment of your imagination. Then, after you write it down, you want to have it available. The more you can read it and even say it aloud, the better. Even just reminding yourself it is there helps, which is where paper comes in really handy.

I keep my electronic notes using Microsoft OneNote. There are other products, but that's the one I have. I can really do anything I want with that product, including photos, copies of e-mails, handwritten notes, typed notes, drawings, and so on. I can create a notebook, and I can put sections in that notebook, and separate pages of notes in each section. It is easy to organize, and I can find any notes I need quickly and easily.

I went to my notebook, opened the folder on health, and then specifically went to the page containing a spell I wrote about a year ago. Here's a problem; just like the CADD system, it took a little while for me to find it. Worse, this is in a notebook I use every day, yet I haven't even seen that page for well over six months. I know it's been over six months since I looked at this particular spell because over six months has passed since I *achieved* that goal. The only reason I found it is because I was *looking* for it. It shouldn't really even be in the notebook. Way worse; it doesn't fit on one screen. Even when I fully zoom out, it's about two screens long. Even with 1080p screen resolution and a 32" monitor, I have the same problem I had back in the old days with the CADD system—I can only see part of it at one time.

What works the best is plain old, three-hole-lined notebook paper, just like you had in school, in a plain old, three-ring binder. If you really want to get fancy, I suppose you could buy some dividers, but I think that's a bit of overkill.

Keep it handy; look it over now and then. The funny thing is that your brain can scan paper *very* fast compared to a computer screen. You read paper differently than you read a computer screen. Study after study confirms that we read paper faster, comprehend the material better, and retain the information better than if we read a screen.[2] Even when you go to review a particular spell (a good idea every now and then, by the way), just paging through the others you might have in the notebook is just going to

---

[2] *International Journal of Educational Research,* Volume 58, 2013, is a recent study.

cement these into your conscious memory, right where you want them.

I often start by typing things out on the computer, just because it is easy to edit and revise. When I get it the way I want it, I read it out loud to hear how it sounds. Finally, I get a sheet of paper, write it out, and put it in the notebook. I read it out loud now and then. If there's something related to the spell that I can keep in view, I do that. For instance, the sales number I mentioned earlier – I wrote that number at the top of a whiteboard I use daily and I left it there to read every day. You might put up a picture where you can see it, or even wallpaper on your computer.

I'm going to summarize the last paragraph, just to make sure you get it. It is *important*.

*Get a sheet of paper and **write it out**. Keep the sheet of paper handy and **read it**. Read it **out loud** now and then. If you can, keep something related in plain view.*

Personalization

Put your name on the piece of paper. You are communicating with your own consciousness, and nothing gets your attention better than hearing your own name.

I used to be a bit stiff about it, by writing, *"I, Michael Ciarochi, will <blah blah blah>"* as though I was repeating some sort of oath. I eventually figured out that I just don't talk that way, and honestly, I don't really listen to anybody that talks that way. Let's be up front about this; *you're talking to yourself!* Okay? So, write to yourself the way you talk to yourself!

This is a matter of getting the attention of your *consciousness*, as we discussed earlier. You are getting your own attention, pointing at this piece of paper and saying, "Look at this! This is what I want!"

Sweat the Small Stuff

As I said in the last chapter, don't overlook the small things in life. Thinking big is great, but the fulfillment of every grand vision is the result of many smaller tasks, and if you don't get those done, the big stuff doesn't happen, either.

A very wealthy individual attributed his financial success to a daily habit of writing down five things that he needed to accomplish that day and not quitting for the day until all five items were done. Basically, he is just creating short-term spells, and there's no law against doing that for things you want to get done *today*. Even at Hogwarts, the kids would just levitate the food right off the serving plate onto their dinner plates.

I think one of the dangers of thinking only big thoughts is that if you let the small stuff pile up you can become overwhelmed with details, and end up losing sight of the big picture. If you just did five things per day, you've accomplished over eighteen hundred things in the course of a year.

How It Looks

We know our magic spell (the technology comes later) is written out, and has the following information:

1. A complete picture of what you want, including:
    a) a clear description of the goal;
    b) what you are going to give up; and
    c) how it will affect your world.
2. A date by when this is going to happen.

We're casting spells here, and some of them last a long time. You don't have to wait for one to finish before starting another, and if you want, you can change the goal at any time. You can nest your spells—say, for an overall, long-term goal for financial independence and cast spells for all of the intermediate steps you need to complete along the way. Anything is *possible*, but it will be a lot more *probable* if you lay down the plan, one step at a time, while you maintain the overall vision of your future. I got the Chevy before I got the dream car. I needed the Chevy to get a job, the job to get a better job leading to a substantial income, after which I could start thinking about a better car. At the same time I was working on my car and finances, I was also working on my health and relationships.

As mentioned earlier, a lot of people want to be wealthy and don't really know what that means. Worse, they have convinced themselves they don't *want* to be wealthy after being inundated day after day with undesirable examples of wealthy, famous, and powerful people. People end up striving to be *poor-but-fulfilled* instead of *wealthy-and-fulfilled*—something that is actually easier to attain. People every day develop a picture of what they want, only to immediately turn around and scribble all over the picture.

- "I want to be famous," followed by
  "but I don't want to have my privacy invaded by paparazzi."
- "I want to be a rock star," followed by
  "but I don't want to be on the road all the time."
- "I want to make a bunch of money," followed by
  "but I don't want to pay all those taxes."
- "I want a promotion," followed by
  "but I don't want the extra work that goes with the job."

- "I want to live at the Country Club," followed by "but I want to keep all my neighborhood friends."

Do you see what that does? Whatever follows the word "but" either completely cancels out the desire or clouds the picture, both in your head *and* in the world. You need to get those objections off the table and out of your head, and the only way you can do that is to *think it through.* Get a solid picture of what you want and what will happen when you get it, and then create the vision of your world the way you want it to be. If you have concerns, incorporate them into your vision in a positive way. For instance, you can change, "I want to be famous but I don't want to have my privacy invaded by paparazzi" to "I will become famous and influential, although my private life will be of little interest to the general public."

While we are on the subject, this isn't just about *things.* This works for relationships, losing weight, or improving your health. Don't overlook any aspect of the world you want to live in. The more you can "see" what you want, the easier it is to believe.

Be as specific as possible when describing what you want. *Truck* is better than vehicle, *pickup truck* is better than truck, and *new, black Ford F-150 Raptor* is better than pickup truck. Get a magazine, cut out pictures of the truck you want, and put them where you'll see them. Go to a dealer and look at it. Sit in it. Think it through and imagine the results—what does driving that truck do for your self-esteem? What are some of the things you can do with it that you can't do now? How will it impact your life?

♦ ♦ ♦ ♦

So what does the spell I'm casting look like? Since I've mentioned weight loss so many times, here's one for that:

<Your name>. By *<specific date>*, I will weigh *<target weight>*. I'll look better, feel better, and be better than ever. In order to get there I'll change my diet and eating habits, losing weight steadily while maintaining optimum health. I have absolute control over my appetite, and I have no desire to consume any foods that will prevent or delay reaching my goal. If I need to, I'll invest time and money for a program that will hold me accountable.

At *<target weight>*, I will be more effective at *<whatever it is you do>*, a better *<spouse/lover/date>*, and an inspiration to my friends and family. I'll be able to wear all of those perfectly good clothes hanging in the closet, and for once I will look forward to putting on a bathing suit and going to the beach. I will enjoy buying new clothes in a size that I can be proud of.

I will continue to learn about diet and nutrition, increasing my health and energy as I lose weight. When I achieve my goal, I will be so delighted with the results that I will naturally strive to maintain my weight and health.

As a point of reference, there is no shortage of weight loss programs. I mentioned Quick Weight Loss Centers of Atlanta. Other proven and popular plans include (in no particular order): Atkins, South Beach, Weight Watchers, NutriSystem, and many, many more. You can find one that will work for you. I suggest that you read reviews of programs, or even better, listen to personal recommendations from people you trust. Talking to people you know who have gotten their weight under control is the best thing possible. Everybody I know who has been successful at this really wants to help others do the same. Ironically, when they help you by making a recommendation, it actually makes them accountable as well. So by asking people how they did it, you are actually helping them, too.

Somebody once asked me what to do if you missed your date. I responded by saying that at one time I had planned on losing twenty pounds by a specific date. When the date arrived, I had lost seventeen pounds. Then I asked if he thought I had failed or succeeded. What do you think?

♦ ♦ ♦ ♦

If you're already skinny, here's one for money:

<your name>. By *<specific date>* I will have *<amount>* *<in the bank/under the mattress/in the cookie jar/in gold>*. This money will accumulate in various amounts from time to time. In return for this money, I'm going to do my best at *<whatever it is you do>*. I will be careful in my spending habits and look for ways to save money wherever possible. I'm also going to sell anything of value that I no longer need using eBay, Craigslist, and other outlets. I will be alert to earning opportunities and will act prudently on those opportunities when they arise.

♦ ♦ ♦ ♦

How about this for a short-term spell?

<your name>. Tomorrow, I'll be driving a clean car. No more stress from driving a dirty car; I'll be proud to be seen in my car. In order to accomplish this, I will go to <name the car wash> and pay using <cash/check/credit card>. While waiting for my car to be washed, I will use my laptop to clean up my e-mail, making efficient use of my time.

Hmmm. . . . Do you need to do little daily spells? The answer is, "It depends."

I mentioned the businessman who, upon arriving at work every day, would simply write down five things he needed to accomplish that day. He put them on an index card and put it in his shirt pocket. Every time he accomplished one of the things, he crossed it off his list and didn't end his day until all five items were completed. "Car wash" is a lot less complicated than writing a short paragraph, and it works. Here's why.

For routine tasks, the visualization is the same from day-to-day, such as relief of stress, feeling good, or advancing your agenda. When you think of washing the car, buying gas, grocery shopping, and many other chores, as soon as you think of the chore, you already know where you are going and how you are going to pay. You have a complete visualization because it's something you've already done. All you really need is a date. In the case of the businessman who used the index card to write down his five tasks, mentioned above, it's only good for one day, so setting the date is done.

In effect, because you already have the complete picture of routine tasks, and the date is implied, the index card is actually a wonderfully efficient way of casting short-term spells and essentially creating your day. It has my highest recommendation as a useful tool. The reason it works is the same reason you would write out any spell. If you only *think* about what you need to do, it never makes it to your memory. You might very well forget something. If you write the list down, you commit it to memory, and by carrying the card with you, you never have to think about what you need to get done. When you cross off an item, you *also* remind yourself what else you need to do, not to mention that just crossing off a task gives you a nice little feeling of accomplishment and positive reinforcement.

I recently heard someone mention that if you go to the store with a shopping list, you not only get everything you needed, but usually a few extras. On the other hand, if you go shopping *without* a list, you might get some stuff you didn't need, but you're likely to forget something that you *did* need. Think of your index card with five tasks as a daily shopping list.

Why then did I say that whether you should write out the paragraph for little daily spells "depends?"

It depends on whether the car wash (or anything else) is routine or not. If it's something you want to develop into a routine, spell it out. If it's something you've done enough times that you don't have to think about it, just jot down a word or two.

Soon, you will associate the necessary steps with almost any task. For instance, after writing down the spell to get the car washed a couple of times, and feeling good about riding in a clean car, and paying for it, your consciousness will automatically associate all of those things with the words "car wash." By creating a daily list, you will also automatically attach a *time* to the list. Thus, you get to the point where you can write, *wash car, mail package, send birthday card* and your memory already has the information necessary to complete the task.

If the task is *not* routine, write it out. Then make a short note on the card referencing the spell you just wrote out (think of it as writing a small spell to invoke another spell).

Write out a new card every day instead of using a notebook or an automated to-do list that rolls everything over. Those tend to get filled up with short-, medium-, and long-term tasks; they get complicated and generally overwhelming. I find that even when I prioritize a "Top Five," I see things further down the list that I'd rather do instead of focusing on the five things I *need* to do. *Keep it short, keep it simple, and keep it fresh.*

A Couple of Additional Notes

What About Setting Goals for Others?

I've given a lot of thought to this. Remember my grandfathers? Their vision created this world for their offspring. Similar stories are playing out throughout the United States by immigrants who came here to create a better life not only for themselves but also for their families. The morality of this is unquestionable, and we all owe a debt to those who created this world for us.

I think that there are some very specific reasons why setting goals for others doesn't always work out. First, you are the center of *your* universe, not the center of somebody else's universe. Theoretically, you can create a world where somebody else achieves success, but then you are still creating a world for *yourself*, not the other person; the other person is just along for the ride, so to speak. This would explain why so many young entertainers completely fall apart when they come of age and start managing their own affairs. Their initial success was actually more the success of their parents or managers than their own. As young stars grow up and assert more control and independence, the direction provided by their handlers becomes less and less influential. Once that driving force that made them successful is reduced to a certain point, things often take a turn for the worse.

That leads right into another issue, which is that this other person *is* in fact the center of his or her universe, and *he* or *she* has his or her own consciousness and control over his or her own life. This person's desires are not very likely to align with yours for very long. This might work temporarily for a young or impressionable person, but eventually he or she will become less focused on pleasing you and more focused on his or her own needs as his or her own consciousness asserts itself.

I had a fellow tell me he wanted to spend his life with a particular woman. They were not together, and the woman wasn't particularly interested in being so. I strongly advised against that course for this reason: you can't really control the consciousness of another person. I recommended that he just focus on finding the perfect partner and let the chips fall where they may. After all, if you find your perfect partner, that pretty much settles the matter. Why would you want a relationship with anybody else, especially somebody who doesn't particularly care that much about you? In fact, by focusing on this particular woman, the fellow may have already missed out on an even better relationship.

It all comes down to focusing your energies where they have the most impact. You have the most impact on *your* world, not somebody else's. This doesn't mean you don't have an impact on the world around you—you do, whether you intend to or not.

I suggest you focus on *your* world and include in your well-conceived vision the many beneficial things that will happen to the rest of your world. Instead of *I want my spouse to lose weight*, you might do better to set a fitness goal for yourself and describe the impact this may have on your spouse: *attaining this goal will serve as an inspiration to my family and friends.*

Instead of *I want to end world hunger,* perhaps by becoming wealthy yourself, you can include: *attaining this goal will allow me to dedicate more time and money toward feeding those in need.*

Instead of *I want my child to be a doctor,* think in terms of becoming successful enough yourself that *attaining my goal will serve as an inspiration to my children and enable me to provide the best of opportunities for them in their chosen endeavors.*

I don't believe my grandfather set a goal for my father to become a pilot and have a successful military career and then go on to run a successful business. In fact, the US Air Force didn't even exist when my grandfather came from Italy. What happened was my grandfather created the *opportunity* for my father and his siblings to create a better life on their own.

It always comes back to you and what you are able to achieve. Go ahead and have a grand vision, but make sure you bring it back to *you* and how *you* can make the grand vision happen.

Hidden Step #4: Do Something

In the first edition of *The Physics of Success*, I failed to mention this – the final step required after you cast your spell and after you commit it to your conscious memory. This final step is that *you are required to do something.*

It's not that I didn't know you had to do something, I just thought it was one of those things that was so obvious that it didn't need mentioning. Silly me.

If you want to lose weight, you need to change what you eat. If you want a new job, you either need to look for a new job or be ready to jump when a new job drops in your lap. If you want your dream companion, you're going to have to say something when you meet.

In short, when opportunity knocks, *open* the door!

♦ ♦ ♦ ♦

There you go; I've told you how to cast a magic spell. What comes next is an explanation of the technology behind the magic.

You can, however, simply start doing this stuff now and it will work.

Remember that this process is about changing your world; it should permeate every single thing that you do. It's like a vegetarian diet—it is different not only from the way you live your life now, it is different from the way most people around you live their lives. If you don't have a solid philosophical or cultural background to support this new habit, you will fall back to the previous "comfortable" thoughts and behaviors.

The following chapters are dedicated to understanding exactly *why* these principles work and how creating and maintaining the image you desire can literally create your future.

Recap

- You are writing things down to get the thought out of the thinking part of your brain and into the remembering part of your brain—your conscious memory.

- Use paper, not an electronic device, to write out your spells. Keep them in a loose leaf notebook.

- Put your name on the paper. Talk to yourself.

- Sweat the small stuff. Write down five things to do on an index card each day. Carry the card with you and don't quit or end your day until you have completed all five items.

- When creating small spells that are not routine, write those out and then note that spell on your index card.

- Remember that while you have a lot of control over your own world, you don't have any control over anybody else's.

- Keep your eyes open to opportunities that lead to the realization of your goals.

- Take action. Nothing is going to happen until you do something.

10

Why Not Psychology?

In the previous chapters on crafting and casting "spells," much of the effectiveness of the techniques can be explained away as simple *psychology*—the study of the human mind. Some people would argue that *everything* can be explained using psychology. Psychology unquestionably plays a very important role in creating your world. People can use autosuggestion or hypnosis to lose weight, quit smoking, or reinforce habits that lead to success. As I described earlier, I wanted a Saab Sonett III at the time I wrote down my statement and slipped it in the book. Even though I forgot about the statement, I still wanted the car, so when an opportunity came to get the car I wanted, I took advantage of the opportunity. Yes, there was a coincidence or two, but coincidence happens all the time. That is easily explained as my mind at work, with no external influences required.

The part about committing an idea to memory by writing it down then reading it back makes sense, but that process is simply an artifact of our brain function. Isn't that reason enough to cause us to change our behavior? Isn't a positive change in behavior sufficient to cause us to effect changes in our lives?

The answer is "yes." If you train yourself to do all of the right things, then you will do very well for yourself. It's been done many times, and it works for a lot of people. The difficulty is what I've mentioned before—using success principles is a different way of life. Without the philosophical understanding that underpins that way of life, it is unlikely that you will maintain the habits of success. Psychology is more of a description than a philosophy. Nonetheless, here are some of the purely psychological explanations for success.

Mental Attitude

Mental attitude includes expectation, belief, and most commonly, positive thinking. This is very important, because casting a spell as described in the previous chapter starts with conception and belief. The very act of casting the spell is setting an expectation; you are describing in detail something that is going to happen and when it is going to happen. Your attitude is not something to easily be dismissed.

However, the appropriate mental attitude is not so much a cause as a *symptom*. It's rather like saying, "If you want to be physically fit, then live a physically active life!" or, "The secret to not being depressed is to be happy!"

It's not so easy to live a physically active life when you are out of shape nor to be happy when you are depressed. It seems that somebody somewhere took a look at very successful people and found they all had a positive attitude with regard to their endeavors. Thus, the conclusion that the positive attitude (or belief, or expectation) is what made the endeavors successful.

I'll let you in on a little secret. Ask any athletic coach – if the team is on a winning streak, it doesn't take a whole lot of effort to pump them up. If they are undefeated and facing a team that has yet to win a game, they will have a very positive attitude about the outcome, and they will believe and totally expect they will win. The coach's challenge will be keeping the team focused on the game and not the postgame celebration.

On the team with the losing record, there's almost nothing you can do other than drill the team on executing strategies to exploit whatever weakness exists on the other team. You make them excited about the new strategies and focus on giving the other team a run for their money. As these strategies begin to work, you will eventually get a win. *Then* the attitude starts to turn around on its own, and the team wants to learn the next new trick that they can use to whomp their next opponent. "Nothing succeeds like success."[1]

In that case, the positive mental attitude starts with being encouraged about new knowledge. It is reinforced by some measure of success. The danger is that expectations may be set too high and the new knowledge might not seem to work; remember, the *other* team has a coach, too, and they also want to win. You need to be careful there is a foundation of substance and realistic expectations underneath the positive attitude. Positive mental attitude (PMA) alone is a rather fragile thing, and the backlash of failure might make matters even worse.

My major objection to positive thinking as a cause is not just that it relies upon human emotion; it actually *is* a human emotion. The same is true for belief and expectation. No offense, but emotions are subject to nearly anything, including the time of year, time of month, day of the week (TGIF!), your health, the balance in your checking account, the mood of your spouse, the mood of your boss, the health of your pet, and on top of all of that,

---

[1] Sir Arthur Helps, *Realmah,* 1868.

even the weather. The phrase "emotional roller coaster" is a very accurate description of the human experience. The question is not whether you're on the roller coaster; it's a question of how scary it is at the moment.

I'm an engineer, and positive thinking never kept a bridge up in the air, and I sure as hell would not want to count on the emotional state of the people building it to assure its integrity. So, I'm not a big fan of positive thinking with respect to getting things done.

I *am* a big fan on doing things that *result* in positive thinking. Understanding how things work is a big step in that direction. Thus, I can determine the structural strength of the raw materials in the design I choose, ensure the contractor tests those materials to confirm they are up to specification, and also that the structure is inspected during critical phases of construction. I can then be very positive about the result; namely, that the bridge will stand no matter what my personal emotional state. The number of bad batches of cement or poor rivets is not relevant, because they were either detected during construction, or my design had sufficient safety factors to accommodate minor flaws of manufacture and construction.

If you are on a team, even if you are down about some aspect of your life, you can still believe the team strategy will work during the big game so long as you do your part.

♦ ♦ ♦ ♦

Along with positive thinking, those same books warn about sabotaging yourself with so-called *negative* thinking. Frankly, there is no such a thing as "positive" or "negative" thinking, per se. It's just thinking. In the previous chapter, I mentioned the necessity of developing a clear picture of your future and also warned you against scribbling all over your picture, using the following as an example:

- "I want to be famous," followed immediately by,
  "But I don't want to have my privacy invaded by paparazzi."

One possible outcome is that the desire for fame might be cancelled by the desire to avoid the attention, and you end up not famous. Another outcome is that you might become famous but have your privacy completely compromised by paparazzi. Either way, the second thought wasn't negative, it was just a thought. If it's on your mind, it's in your picture. It's not a negative picture; it's just not the picture you *want.* The combined result of both thoughts was simply a less-than-desirable destination. By developing a different image that incorporates your fear in a desirable manner, as in, "I will become famous and influential, although my private life will be of little interest to the general public," you attain the desired result, including avoiding the matters of concern.

Some of the teachings using positive mental attitude strongly emphasize the avoidance of *any* negativity in your life. I understand this and agree that our environment can have a tremendous influence on our beliefs. Obviously, you should strive to surround yourself with a supportive environment. However, your environment might not be as cooperative as you like. Again, you choose to do things that *result* in positive thinking. An engineer who is very unhappy with his employer can still design a perfectly good bridge. A player on a losing team can execute his job on the team flawlessly, creating confidence in other team members.

If you begin to feel the world is against you, go back and read the chapter on "Accountability" again and remind yourself who has the most influence on your world.

The Subconscious Mind

Some of you might have noticed that I don't use the word "subconscious" very often, if at all. To me, it's the cloud in the formula containing the phrase, "A miracle happens here."

I haven't read all of the books on self-improvement or success by any stretch of the imagination. It seems a lot, if not the majority, of the ones I *have* read make use of the subconscious mind (or its equivalent) as an explanation for the "magic" that seems to happen.

Essentially, the subconscious mind (universal mind, the "I AM", or cosmic all) is super powerful, but we do not harness it for some reason or another (negative feelings, bad vibrations, the souls of evil aliens[2]). All you need to do is, somehow or other, pound the good things into your conscious mind hard enough that it gets through to your subconscious mind, which then takes over and wonderful things happen.

That is all well and good, and for all I know, might very well represent what happens. There are some inconsistencies, and those, as you know by now, really bother me.

First and foremost, the subconscious mind seems to minimize our conscious minds. If you recall my earlier discussion, your conscious mind is absolutely amazing. Our awareness of our universe, our ability to predict the future, and our ability to deliberately act in specific ways to affect the future (also known

---

[2] You know who you are.

as free will) is unparalleled in nature. If our conscious minds were actually a filter standing *in the way* of the pure actions of our subconscious minds, then animals would reign supreme and there would be no use for mankind. If we existed, we would be quite far down the evolutionary ladder. Our complicated thoughts would be getting in the way of everything. Animals, with their relatively simple consciousness, would instinctively instruct their subconscious minds to create an ideal world for themselves.

Another problem is the idea that the subconscious mind has all this power but seems to be completely ignorant—much like a powerful robot with no self-guiding intelligence. I question why something so stupid with that much apparent power even exists. In the hierarchy of life, the more powerful awareness and consciousness a creature has, the more apparent it is. It's not something that remains hidden from the creature waiting to be discovered. A shark can smell blood in the water a mile away, and we know it can because if you drop blood in the water, sharks come from a mile around. A cheetah can run fast, and we know it can run fast because it *runs fast.* Humans are intelligent, and we know that because we are conspicuously *smart.* Sharks don't swim around aimlessly, a cheetah doesn't just mosey along after a herd of gazelle, and humans don't just sit there acting stupid all the time (only *part* of the time). Why would we have an amazing subconscious mind that doesn't do anything and has no outward manifestation?

Alternatively, a "higher" consciousness is substituted for the subconscious in this context, but it basically works the same. In some cases, it is still called the subconscious; in some cases, it actually takes the form of a consciousness in a spiritual realm. I have even more problems with this concept—if we have a separate *and* intelligent spiritual consciousness, why does it sit there doing nothing while the physical manifestation of this spirit is suffering? That simply makes no sense.

Finally, in actual practice, psychologists don't refer to the subconscious mind as a separate entity as described by many success methods. Sigmund Freud once said:

> "If someone talks of subconsciousness, I cannot tell whether he means the term topographically—to indicate something lying in the mind beneath consciousness—or qualitatively – to indicate another consciousness, a subterranean one, as it were. He is probably not clear about any of it. The only trustworthy antithesis is between conscious and unconscious."[3]

In practice, psychologists usually refer to the *unconscious* mind to avoid the confusion described by Freud. They are generally referring to autonomous functions (such as the beating of your heart, breathing, digestion, etc.) as well as memory, habit, and instinct, all of which are outside the realm of consciousness.

I believe that the reason the subconscious mind is so predominant in self-help literature dates back to Napoleon Hill's *Think and Grow Rich*, which is the first and perhaps most widely read of modern success methods (1937). In the book, Napoleon Hill refers to autosuggestion, which technique in turn dates to the early 1900s. Émile Coué was an apothecary who was very curious about the placebo effect.[4] Émile turned to hypnosis; hypnotic suggestion had the same general effect as the placebo,

---

[3] Sigmund Freud, *The Question of Lay Analysis* (Vienna 1926; English translation 1927).

[4] Where a cure is effected in a patient when given a medically ineffective treatment (such as a sugar pill).

but the effect diminished as the patient regained consciousness. He then concluded that a patient could essentially self-induce a hypnotic suggestion, and this "autosuggestion" would persist because it was created internally instead of the suggestion coming from an outside source. Émile got the idea of implanting the suggestion in this undefined "subconscious" mind from hypnosis, and Napoleon Hill adopted autosuggestion and the subconscious mind from Émile Coué to explain the effects of his success principles. I think it highly likely that many authors adopted Napoleon Hill's explanation. However, as I described earlier, the entire concept of the subconscious mind as a "subterranean" mind not only doesn't make sense, it was not and still is not accepted as a medical fact.

Focus

To demonstrate focus to yourself, just close your eyes and name as many blue objects as you can in the room without looking around (go ahead, do it!). You may be able to name one or two things, but after opening your eyes, you will see more blue things around you than you thought. This *focus* is what is at play when you buy a new car and suddenly you notice all of the other cars like yours on the road. If you become pregnant, suddenly it seems like there are a lot of pregnant women out there, not to mention maternity stores you never noticed before.

When your conscious mind is focused on something, your attention is drawn to anything related to that thing. That's one way to explain why I noticed the wrecked Sonett being towed, why I followed it and determined: (a) it could be repaired, and (b) it was cheap enough that repairing it would be worth the investment. I probably saw several cars being towed, but because they were not Sonetts, I paid no attention.

Focus will also cause you to move yourself into situations that will promote your cause. If you seek a mate, you are more likely to go to places where you might find a suitable mate. If you are looking for a car, you may visit showrooms or pay close attention to automobile commercials.[5]

Focus is indeed a powerful factor and might be sufficient to explain everything to some people on brief examination. Using focus as a pure psychological explanation, you can argue that opportunities *seem* to be more available because we are looking for opportunities. What appear to be serendipitous coincidences are really there all of the time, but we simply notice them because we are *looking* for them. However, if you employ success principles for very long, serendipity stops being serendipitous and becomes a way of life. The strings of coincidence leading to success tend to get very long and convoluted. You might say it starts to look like magic. Increasingly, there seems to be some additional factor at play assisting in the success of some individuals.

The Conscious Mind

If I rule out a subconscious mind or a higher consciousness, then I'm pretty much stuck with the conscious mind. Here's where we step into a real bucket of manure.

As far as I know, nobody has ever figured out *what it is.*

---

[5] If you're broke, you might pay close attention to tow trucks.

We can measure it. We can make it go away. In some cases, we can even bring it back.[6] We have a lot of analogies to describe it, and each and every person reading this book experiences it; but in the end, we have absolutely no idea what it is.

That's a real stinker, and the greatest minds in the world[7] have yet to do any better than, "I think, therefore I am."

It's not because nobody bothered to look. Scientists and doctors have looked all over the place for it, and haven't found it. We've mapped the brain and studied all of its functions. We can say, "Here is the speech center," "Here is where the sense of smell is processed," or "This is the part that makes your left index finger twitch," but there is no chart with an arrow pointing to the location of consciousness. Some conscious animals such as insects have brains that are radically different than ours.

We know we can *alter* consciousness by physically manipulating the brain and have evidence that certain personality characteristics can be associated with specific physical brain abnormalities. However, we just can't quite pinpoint who it is looking out of our eyes.

♦ ♦ ♦ ♦

This is a good time to discuss an artifact of consciousness. As a conscious being, you look out through your eyes. You listen with your ears. You smell with your nose, touch with your skin, and taste with your tongue. Let's focus on vision for a moment.

---

[6] Actually, I'm not sure we can make it go away. I was thinking of anesthesia, but I believe anesthesia shuts down your *awareness*, or sensory input. Rather like unhooking the I/O bus of a computer—if the CPU has no input, it's just sits there doing nothing even if it is still turned on.

[7] Even Bomb #20!

We talk about looking at something as though it is an activity that we do. I remember my kids as toddlers having a fight in the backseat of the car and one of them yelling, "He's looking out my window!"

It sounds silly to an adult, but you and I are guilty of the same silliness every day. The children treated the act of looking as something that we *do*. However, the physical reality is we are simply pointing our light sensors in a particular direction. Everything we see comes from the *outside in*. Yet we universally perceive this to be opposite. I say (and feel) that I just looked out the window. In truth, all I did was aim my pupils at the window. In fact, because the window is in front of my desk as I type this, I don't really have to move my eyes at all. The light from the window is already entering my eyeballs.

This might sound a bit irrelevant, but it is a critical piece to understanding consciousness. When I look out the window, I am *not* "aiming my pupils" out the window. I am *directing my consciousness* to the world outside my window. When I look out the window, I can see the computer screen (the screen actually covers the bottom portion of the window). If I "aim my pupils" to a point just over the top of the screen, I can see the arch of a window of the house across the street. Even if I force my eyes to focus at the distance of the screen[8], *I cannot read the clearly visible text.* Believe me, I tried. Maybe if I kept at it a while, I could manage, but it just isn't worth the effort. If I want to read the text on the screen, I have to aim my pupils at the screen.

As I tried this, it became apparent that the amount of my visual field actually occupying my *consciousness* is pretty tiny! I can

---

[8] This technique is similar to focusing on patterns containing embedded 3-D images.

look at my screen and see fall colors out the window in a general way. I can look at the same spot and also see a messy desk and a piece of paper just under the screen. However, if I want to *see* the trees I have to look out the window. Then I see several different trees in various states of fall fashion. If I want to see what the paper is, I have to look at it.

This is an important distinction between *awareness* and *consciousness.* Vertically in my visual field I am aware of (from bottom to top) a yellow piece of paper, the computer screen, and the window. I am *aware* of them all. However, I can direct my consciousness toward only one at a time.

I may be typing away at the text with my consciousness focused on the screen, and the cat (bless his heart) might knock something off the desk. My consciousness will reflexively re-focus and (attempt to) keep the something from falling or breaking. This awareness of motion within our field of vision is a natural survival instinct. It is not learned.[9]

When we examine consciousness and awareness, it appears our awareness is broad and general, where consciousness is narrow and focused. It's the "narrow and focused" part that we cannot find in our minds. If we simply had awareness without consciousness, I would just sit here and "take in" whatever

---

[9] You can make yourself a safer driver by being aware of this human instinct. A lot of motorcyclists know it is dangerous to drive the same speed as surrounding traffic. If there is no relative motion between them and a car, the driver of the car will not see them because (a) the driver is mostly expecting other *cars* on the road, and (b) without any relative motion, the motorcycle just becomes part of the background. However, if the motorcycle is overtaking the car, the motion caught in the mirror or peripheral vision of the car driver will attract the driver's attention (consciousness). This is also true for driving a car in somebody's blind spot. Relative motion will attract the conscious attention of other drivers.

sensory input the world threw at me. The phrase *vegetative state* comes to mind.

We can calculate the ability of the eye to see and the ear to hear. We can examine and quantify all of the sensory input that makes up our awareness of our world. We cannot do the same for consciousness; it's something entirely different. When my daughter yelled, "He's looking out my window!" she knew exactly what she was talking about – namely, her brother was intentionally invading her space with his consciousness. She just didn't have the necessary vocabulary at the time to describe what was going on.

This brings us full circle back to our persistent feeling that we are *looking from the "inside-out,"* when, in fact, we are actually receiving information from the *"outside-in."* That's because when we talk about seeing (or listening, tasting, smelling, or feeling) something, we are talking about our consciousness, not our awareness. It is why two people sitting next to each other in an auditorium can have completely different experiences. This part of ourselves that we *recognize* as ourselves is the same part we have yet to identify – the human consciousness.

Why Not Psychology?

In the long run, psychology may *describe* what is going on, but it is simply unable to provide a comprehensive *explanation* for what is going on. The primary activity is *focus*; if we focus our consciousness using the written and spoken word, and hold clear and persistent images of our desire, then our consciousness will direct our actions toward the attainment of that desire. The physics of consciousness described in the following chapters also use focus, because the idea is that the conscious mind is the driving force behind what happens in our lives.

The biggest problems with psychology as the complete explanation are that it does not explain the long chain of serendipitous events associated with success, and if the *desire itself* is generated in our consciousness, why do we need to tell our consciousness something that started out as its own idea?

At this point, we can look toward physics. There literally *has* to be a physical explanation if for no other reason than we know the process works.

Recap

- Psychology *can* provide explanation enough for some people, but does not provide a philosophy to support the adoption of success principles as a way of life.

- Mental attitude (including belief and positive thinking) are symptoms rather than causes. What really matters is the confidence that your correct *actions* will eventually result in correct results.

- The subconscious (or some sort of superconscious) mind doesn't really exist as a discrete brain function. There is no logic behind the assumption that such a thing has anything to do with your success.

- Although its existence is self-evident, the conscious mind has yet to be mapped; scientists have not been able to pinpoint its functional location in either man or animal. Although our awareness through our sensory input is very comprehensive and general, our conscious awareness is very specific and limited.

- Although our sensory input comes from the "outside in," we think of our consciousness as being from the "inside out" (we thing of looking *out at* something, when, in fact, all we physically do is point our eyes at it).

11

Why Physics?

"Physics" is the science of nature, with a particular focus on matter and energy (which Einstein so inconveniently theorized to be equivalent, a theory that has been confirmed many times). Anything that exists is subject to the laws of physics. This includes silly things like gravity and electricity, neither of which is entirely comprehensible even though we understand how they both work pretty thoroughly.

When you compare the definitions of physics and "philosophy" (which is "the study of the fundamental nature of knowledge, reality, and existence"), you find a lot of common ground; physics is a subset of philosophy. The common themes between the two have been noted many times by many authors. Physics must include an explanation of life and consciousness, and furthermore, that immeasurable part of us that goes away when we die. I say it *must* because the existence of consciousness is, as our comrade Bomb #20 says, "Intuitively obvious."

Because consciousness exists, it must have an explanation in physics.

Why Physics?

The main title of this book is *The Physics of Success,* so I obviously need to address the subject. Aside from that obvious fact, "physics" is not just a word I used to catch your attention; it is the fundamental reason this book exists. The remaining chapters are intended to change your understanding of the physical universe and subsequently change your behavior based on that new knowledge. The idea is that your new behavior will change your world from a place where you *happen to be* into a place that you *created for yourself.*

There are two obvious reasons to read a book called *The Physics of Success.* One is that you want to learn more about physics and are interested in this particular explanation. The second is that you want to learn more about success and are interested in this particular application.

If the first approach describes you, this is where things start to get interesting. On the other hand it's more likely that you're more interested in success than in physics, so for you this is where things become a bit challenging. This is not to say that you find the topic of physics uninteresting, just that it might be somewhat out of your comfort zone.

That's a *good* thing. If you know anything at all, you know that to excel at anything, you need to move out of your comfort zone. If it helps, imagine yourself as Queen Isabella of Spain listening to the arguments of Christopher Columbus as he petitions you to fund an expedition to sail *westward* in order to reach the *Far East.* It will require some thinking on your part. A certain hesitation to accept new ideas is only to be expected, but the results can be extraordinary.

♦ ♦ ♦ ♦

After reading this far, you should have a good start toward creating the world you want to live in. It's a world limited only by your imagination and your ability to *convince yourself* that the world of your imagination can come to pass. You have rules to follow in order to *focus* your desire, envision the result, and get the attention of your consciousness. When you create the complete picture of what you want and write it down so you can maintain the image in your mind, you have greatly increased the chances of bringing that reality to existence in your universe.

If you're paying really close attention, you should be thinking something along the order of, "Hey! Wait a minute! You said this would work, and now you're saying it increases my *chances?*"

Yes. Remember Harry Potter? Why does Harry Potter, with all of his abilities, have problems? He has problems because there are other people in his world with every bit as much (or more) power and every bit as much (or more) knowledge who oppose him. Remember the world where everybody is a wizard, but nobody bothered to tell them?

You may be the center of your universe, and you may have the most influence in *your* universe, but you are sharing your universe with billions of other conscious beings, and each and every one of them has the same ability to shape that universe. Your universe overlaps the universes of people around you. Thus, when they shape *their* world, it shapes *your* world as well. Good thing, too, or there would be no bread for you on the shelves of the grocery store. There wouldn't be a grocery store, for that matter.

That means you can't simply write down *I wanna win the lottery* and win it (although it wouldn't hurt your chances). You happen to be sharing the lottery with a boatload of other people, and guess how many of them want to win the lottery? Not only that, there's a whole mess of people out there who *didn't* buy a ticket but are imagining themselves picking up a winning ticket that some idiot dropped or threw away! To make matters worse, there are people out there who play the lottery using a system, which is going to increase *their* chances for no other reason than they are following the same rules you are following, even if it is just by accident. And then there are people out there praying, and thinking positive, not to mention quite a number of them doing exactly what you are doing.

That's a lot of competition. If they had a lottery in Harry Potter's world, can you imagine the magic that would be flying all over the place? Wizards predicting which numbers would be drawn; Wizards casting spells to influence the draw, Wizards casting spells on the tickets to make them winners; Wizards casting spells on other Wizards' tickets to make them losers; and so on. The place would probably just go **poof** in some kind of magical short circuit.

As you know by now, inconsistency bothers me. There are other forces out there, and the failure to account for that fact is an inconsistency in a lot of success methods. They *work* because they make use of basic principles. However, sooner or later, you *will* run into other people who are just as determined as you and are competing for the same resource. Eventually, you will miss the mark, and your confidence in the process is damaged. Furthermore, the combined effort and belief of billions of other beings have already set many things in motion, and it would be a great challenge to stop those things. Perhaps you absolutely *hate* mobile phones. Well, good luck trying to get them out of your world. You might have to relocate the center of your universe to the middle of Antarctica.

To make things perfectly clear, this is about increasing your odds. If you get good enough at this, it increases your odds to the point that it seems like magic. Think of this process as learning to sail a boat. You can put a boat out to sea, and it will be completely at the mercy of the current. You can make a paddle and work very hard, but the current will still dominate the direction you're traveling. You can put up a sail, and now you will be at the mercy of the wind and the current; the paddle is still comparatively ineffective. What I am suggesting is that you drop a keel into the sea, put a sail up into the wind, and use the paddle as a rudder. Suddenly, you have much more control over the direction of your boat; you're not only doing less work, you're a lot more likely to end up where you want to go.

As you learn to sail, you make adjustments to your boat, the keel, the rudder, and the sail. You will learn to tack against the wind and will soon be able to guide your boat exactly where you want it to go. Does that mean you have 100 percent control? No, the wind may die or there may be a storm. But in all conditions, you will be far better off knowing how to sail than just sitting in a boat entirely at the mercy of the wind and the current.

In this case, the sea is your world, and the current, waves, and wind are probabilities. These have direct analogies in the world of physics, and your ability to manage the probabilities in your world will determine what your world will be. Thus, we talk about physics.

The M(*x*)croscopic Universe

The universe is huge; it is enormous beyond our capacity to imagine. We can't imagine the size of the planet on which we live, and it is just a small planet in our solar system. We cannot envision the size of the sun, and it's a relatively small star in our galaxy of some four hundred billion (4×10^{11}) stars, which is one of several hundred billion galaxies. That's the "Macroscopic Universe."

Tiny beyond the threshold of visibility, and beyond even the threshold of the visible light spectrum, are molecular, atomic, and subatomic particles. There are so many of them it is beyond our ability to imagine. Each of us is a colony of approximately ten trillion (10×10^{12}) cells, yet *each* of our trillions of cells is composed of approximately seven trillion *trillion* (7×10^{27}) individual atoms[1], and each atom is composed of a variety of subatomic particles. We cannot envision the composition of a single tiny cell. That's the "Microscopic Universe."

In the microscopic universe, we find that within the densest matter, there is actually more space than particles. After learning about atoms as a child, with their electrons in orbit around their nuclei, I imagined that Earth was just an electron, the solar system an atom, and the Milky Way a molecule that made up some incredibly huge thing. Maybe I was part of an atom in a molecule that was part of a cell that made up some incredibly huge kid who was looking up into *his* sky and wondering the same thing. Maybe there were millions of subatomic-sized kids on the atoms inside of *me* doing the same thing.

If you *could* stand on one of those subatomic particles, the cell *would* seem to be the size of the universe that you now see when you look into the sky. There are trillions of cells in your body,

---

[1] Hydrogen, oxygen, and carbon make up about 99 percent of the human body. Assuming an average adult weighs 70 kilograms, the count is approximately 4.7×10^{27} hydrogen atoms, 1.8×10^{27} oxygen atoms, and 7.0×10^{26} carbon atoms, for a total of a little more than 7×10^{27} atoms.

billions of bodies in the world, and yet all of the people in the world combined are not even 14 trillionths of the mass of Earth.[2]

It's worth taking a few minutes to contemplate both how big the universe is on the *outside* (the macroscopic universe) and also the apparent fact that it is just as big on the *inside* (the microscopic universe). It is important for you to understand that there is a lot of room in the universe, scaling in both directions, and there is a lot of stuff going on that you are not aware of. We simply don't have sufficient sensory apparatus. When we build machines to see things we cannot see, whether it is the Hubble Telescope, an electron scanning microscope, or even our mobile phone, we are enhancing our sensory input to allow our consciousness to focus in ways we are not naturally able to do, and, in effect, expanding the reach of our consciousness into the universe.

It is the struggle of physics to explain the *entire* universe, large and small. It is a fascinating subject and requires an intellect and dedication beyond what I have devoted to the subject. However, I have a few insights based on some of the information that I have managed to understand.

Keep Your Eye on the Cat

There is a phenomenon called the *observer effect*. This refers to the fact that the act of observation changes the behavior of what is being observed. It applies to almost anything. In physics, the tools used to measure something affect what is being measured. For

---

[2] The average adult male is 70 kilograms and the average adult female is just over 61 kilograms, averaging about 65 kilograms per person. 6.5 billion people times 65 kilograms equals 422.5 billion kilograms (4.2×10^{11}). Divided into the mass of Earth (6×10^{24} kilograms), the mass of humanity is 14 trillionths the mass of Earth (1/14,201,183,431,953).

instance, a thermometer will transfer heat to or from whatever you are using the thermometer to measure. A well-designed experiment takes this into account. In some cases, there is negligible effect; for instance, using a thermometer to measure the temperature outside is not going to change the weather. In other cases, the effects can be very complex and cannot be extracted from an experiment.

This is the case with the observer effect in quantum mechanics. The Heisenberg uncertainty principle is based on the observer effect and states, among other things, that it is not possible to precisely know both the velocity and position of a particle. Measuring one of the properties interferes with your ability to accurately measure the other property. Particles exist as a probability (known as *quantum superposition*) until one of its properties is observed, at which point the wave function describing the probability curve collapses into one particular state for the particle being observed. The observer effect is quite well known for the part it plays in the thought experiment known as Schrödinger's cat. It's a fascinating discussion, with a rather dry humor about the whole thing. It goes like this (at least *my* version does):

In 1935, physicist Erwin Schrödinger proposed an experiment in which you place a cat in a box containing a rather clever device. This device, which he called a *diabolical mechanism,* consists of a small bit of radioactive material, a Geiger counter, a relay, a small hammer, and a sealed flask containing hydrocyanic acid. It is rigged up in such a way that at some random time during the course of a day, a radioactive particle activates the Geiger counter, which then triggers the relay, in turn releasing the hammer that breaks the flask, which releases the poison that subsequently kills the cat.[3]

The thought experiment is intended to illustrate a paradox regarding quantum superposition. According to the theory of quantum superposition, the cat would be both alive *and* dead at the same time, until you actually opened the box, at which point the waveforms would collapse to one or the other reality—live cat or dead cat. To quote Herr Schrödinger, "The psi-function of the entire system would express this by having in it the living and dead cat (pardon the expression) mixed or smeared out in equal parts."[4]

I like the way this guy thinks!

Of course, the cat knows if it's dead—well, at least it would know if it's *alive*. It can't really be both, can it?

Schrödinger proposed this experiment in 1935 and never harmed a cat to my knowledge. The experiment is an excellent exercise more than seventy years later. It's still famous because the answer is *not* straightforward. The closest thing we have to a philosophical parallel is the question, "If a tree falls in the forest, and there is nobody around to hear, does it make a sound?"

The situations with the cat and the tree both sound a bit silly, but are still discussed with absolute seriousness. What's really interesting about Schrödinger's cat is that it raises the question of the cat being the observer. Until then, it was pretty easy to simply say, "If a particle could be in one of two states, it exists as a

---

[3] Erwin Schrödinger and Rube Goldberg were both alive at the same time, and the diabolical contraption makes me wonder if they knew each other and collaborated on the design.

[4] Naturwissenschaften ("Natural Sciences") in 1935.

probability of either state until you actually look at it, then the wave function collapses into one state or the other."

This is not a problem because the particle can't observe its own state, so who cares? The same is true for the tree. The cat, on the other hand, is fully aware of looking at itself, licking itself, or chasing its own tail if it so pleases. What happens to your wave function then, Mr. Physicist? Is that meowing noise coming out of your diabolical contraption a live cat or the ghost of a dead cat? That paradox was part of the genius of the experiment; introducing the concept that what is happening in the microscopic universe (the decay of a radioactive atomic particle) actually *does* affect the macroscopic universe (namely the cat), and you can't simply ignore one of them for the convenience of mathematics.

The observer effect in this context is very relevant and important to you. Remember, you are literally the center of this incredibly large (and small) universe, and you take it with you wherever you go. When you do something in your world, it changes literally *everything* you perceive with your senses.

Think of yourself as the cat and the universe as the box. We'll be coming back to this.

Dimensions

You, Bomb #20, and I obtain sensory input from three dimensions: height, width, and depth; that's what we can see and touch. We also are aware of the passage of time, which is considered to be a fourth dimension since Einstein included it as such with his theories of relativity. The three "spatial" dimensions are: height, width, and depth. You and I can move through these with relative ease; we can move forward and back, side to side, up and down, and any combination of these. Time seems to be a bit of a stinker in that we just seem to be along for the ride, so to speak. We can't go forward and back in time, only forward. In a sense, it seems like perhaps we just don't have the right kind of *flippers* or whatever appendage is required to move through that dimension; we're just floating along down the river of time along with all the other flotsam. Einstein demonstrated with his theory of relativity that space and time are one and the same (*spacetime*), but for purposes here, I'm going to refer to height, width, and depth as the "spatial" dimensions. As far as our senses go, this is an adequate description.

Interestingly, while we have our five senses contributing to the detection of height, width, and depth, we don't have anything that directly detects the passage of time. We can hear sound, make an educated guess as to whether it is close or far away, and in what direction. We can follow our nose into the kitchen, and so on. If you really think about it, the only thing that makes us aware of time at all is our consciousness; to be aware of time, we must *think* about it. The only way we can use our conscious awareness of time to our advantage is by *thinking* with our *consciousness* (e.g., I toss the cat in the garage when I'm putting the groceries away).[5] This is a rather important point, so don't forget it. Our senses (sight, sound, taste, touch, and smell) all give us a *spatial* reference. Only our consciousness gives us a temporal reference. *We have no sensory apparatus to detect time.*

---

[5] We have two eyes for the purpose of developing a three-dimensional stereoscopic view of three dimensions. According to the theories of relativity, time is also different from different observational points, just as it is in spatial dimensions. I wonder: if we had two conscious viewpoints in two different places that reported to a single consciousness, would we then be able to mentally assemble a four-dimensional view of the universe?

♦ ♦ ♦ ♦

Physicists theorize there are likely to be eleven or more dimensions. (There are books written for the lay person that describe these, notably *Hyperspace* by Michio Kaku and *The Elegant Universe* by Brian Greene. If you are interested in the world around you, get these books and read them. These excellent books and others already exist, and in order to do justice to the subject, you *need* something at least as long as a book, so I'm not going to attempt to provide a comprehensive explanation here. You either need to take my word for it or get the books and read them for yourself.)

The concept of dimensions, in addition to the ones we can directly observe, predates Einstein by a long time. Humans have been envisioning an alternative dimension (or parallel universe) in stories for thousands of years. They have been proposed as the location of the underworld, heaven, Faerie, and, of course, the place where ghosts seem to get stuck. This was not just promoted by folklore, but actually incorporated by religion to explain why we can't see God (or the gods)—they all live in the "spiritual plane" of existence. A great deal of legitimate scientific effort has been expended searching for gateways into alternate dimensions.

These other places, worlds, or universes are often referred to as "alternate dimensions." This is because for all intents and purposes, a world we cannot see is either far away on another planet or it *must* exist in a different and additional dimension. If we *could* see it, we *would* see it, and if it existed here in our three spatial dimensions on the planet Earth, we could see it.

Time is also another dimension and is an interesting topic. Everything we observe is in the past. Even talking face-to-face with somebody, it took the light and sound a fraction of a second to travel to your eyes and ears. When we look to the sky, everything we see is in the objects' past; in the case of stars, we are observing the stars as they were many years ago, because it takes time for the light to reach Earth. For all we know, our galaxy blew up a few years ago. There is no way for us to tell until the information (traveling at the speed of light) reaches us. We have absolutely no idea what the universe looks like *right now* because all of the electromagnetic information that we use to observe the cosmos arrives at different time references. Light from the sun is about eight seconds old; from the nearest star (Alpha Centauri) is over four *years* old; the nearest galaxy, (Andromeda) over two and a half *million* years old; and the farthest confirmed galaxy (IOK-1), over twelve *billion* years old. When you look into the night sky (or look anywhere, for that matter), you are seeing things as they were at various times in the *past*. We literally do not know what the universe looks like at this moment; we could only guess, and it would not even be a very good guess.

There is speculation that there are unseen worlds sharing our universe that are slightly offset in time. This is used as a possible explanation of many of our myths and folktales. Considering that *everything* we observe is, in fact, offset in time to some degree, it's highly unlikely this is the case. If it shares our three-dimensional universe, we will either see it directly or see artifacts of its existence. If we cannot observe something or see artifacts of its existence, it is highly unlikely it shares our measurable universe and must therefore exist in a dimensional structure beyond the four dimensions we can measure.[6]

♦ ♦ ♦ ♦

Back to topic. Philosophers, theologians, and physicists were all looking for alternate dimensions prior to Einstein. Einstein was the first to demonstrate that time was inextricably tied to the three commonly accepted spatial dimensions and therefore considered a fourth dimension.

This led to a bit of a dilemma because a lot of people were speculating about a fourth dimension. When Einstein pointed out the fourth dimension was time, it kind of screwed up how everybody was counting dimensions. Everybody already *knew* about time, that was not what they meant by the "fourth dimension."

I mention this only because prior to Einstein, there were some pretty good mathematical foundations laid for the inclusion of a fifth dimension, except everybody was calling it the *fourth* dimension. Oops.

What a Dimension *Really* Represents

When the post office asks the dimensions of your parcel, they aren't asking whether the parcel is in this universe or the universe of Faerie (I checked, and they cannot deliver to that address). They are asking you about the height, width, and depth of the parcel.

---

[6] It's very interesting that many legends, such as travel to Faerie or the story of Rip Van Winkle, describe time dilation, usually with the hero returning to their normal world only to find everybody had grown much older during the hero's brief sojourn. These legends predate Einstein by quite a bit but are fascinating because they describe relativistic phenomenon very accurately.

A place, whether it is Faerie or your house, is not a dimension. A place is a location. Traditionally, we think of a place as described in three dimensions, generally given in x, y, and z coordinates, but that isn't entirely accurate. Consider an example:

> We agree to meet for coffee. What is the next step? Namely, *where* are we going to meet for coffee? In America, you can get coffee practically anywhere.
>
> So, we agree to meet for coffee at Starbuck's. Okay, that narrows it down to about 20,000+ possible locations, because in America, Starbuck's is just about everywhere.[7]
>
> Okay, we agree to meet at the Starbuck's at the corner of Main and Elm Streets in our town. That pretty much eliminates all but one of the Starbuck's in the world, so we should be good, right? Is there anything missing?
>
> You bet. What is missing is *what time* are we going to meet at the Starbuck's on the corner of Main and Elm Streets in our town?

Here is what happened. We located the x, y, and z coordinates of the particular store for our meeting. If z is the vertical dimension, it is implied that the building with that store is actually on the ground (I haven't seen any floating buildings, at least in my town). The corner of Main and Elm Streets is actually an intersection of x and y dimensions. So, we have nailed down the three-dimensional location of our store.

However, in order to complete the location of our meeting, we need to provide a measurement in a *fourth* dimension, namely time; say, 2:00 p.m. next Thursday.

---

[7] Except when you really want one they seem really hard to find.

So, the coffee shop is the place, but the location of the *meeting* where we are having coffee is described by measurements along the *x, y, z,* and *w* dimensions. A dimension is not a place. A dimension is a *direction,* and we can locate a place by measuring along a certain direction (aka, dimension).

Why Do We Need More than Three (er, *Four*) Dimensions Anyway?

One of the earliest struggles I had with physics was way back in school when we studied properties of light, particularly the part where light behaves as though it were both a particle and a wave. I know now there are perfectly good reasons demonstrated in quantum mechanics for this apparent paradox, but this was before we got to the chapter on quantum mechanics, so the damage had been done. This unanswered question ultimately led to why I asked a Fermilab physicist about electricity. There are several variations of the question, but here are a few:

- How does a light wave get to Earth from the sun, if there is nothing to "wave" through in the vacuum of space? *[The original question]*

- We sent guys to the moon, and we sent TV and radio signals back-and-forth through the vacuum of space; how did the radio and TV signals do that if there is nothing to "wave" in a vacuum?

- If there are photons involved in radio transmissions, why can't I see those photons?

- If a vacuum is such a good insulator, how does the heat from the sun get here?

- Why does light travel the same speed everywhere, all of the time?

- Why is the speed of light and the speed of an electric current essentially the same, even though they are completely different things (photons waving through a vacuum vs electrons waving back-and-forth in copper)?

And so on. Fortunately, my teacher liked me (not all of them did). She was probably very happy I never got around to thinking about gravity during her class.

Einstein was able to mathematically eliminate certain apparent paradoxes in our universe by incorporating *time* as another dimension in addition to the three spatial dimensions. This introduction of an additional dimension explained a lot of problematic questions. One of Einstein's greatest challenges was to mathematically unite the behaviors of light and *gravity*. Einstein was unable to do this until he received a paper from a physicist named Theodr Kaluza who proposed the addition of a *fifth* dimension to Einstein's four-dimensional equations, into which the equations of both light and gravity fit perfectly.

You may read about these events in the some of the titles mentioned in the "Recommended Reading" section at the end of this book. Instead of making things more complicated, the addition of another dimension made things *less* complicated. The big problem with more than three dimensions is we don't have the *sensory apparatus* to detect anything in the fifth, sixth, or any other dimension. Remember, we don't even have sensory apparatus to detect the passage of time; we need to *think* about it. We can only conclude that in order for certain things to happen in the dimensions we *can* observe, it makes sense there are additional dimensions.

The next problem physicists encountered (and there always is a next problem) was that a new branch of physics, *quantum mechanics,* was having fantastic theoretical and practical success. Your mobile phone is possible only through the practical application of quantum mechanics. This is a problem because quantum mechanics, which works very well in the microscopic universe, and general relativity, which works very well in the macroscopic universe, were, for the most part, completely incompatible—quantum mechanics has problems on large scales, and relativity has problems on small scales. Since scientists usually work either on large scales or small scales, there is no practical issue at stake. We can make a cell phone, and we can land a remote-controlled robot on Mars. No problem. However, that kind of inconsistency is the sort of thing that would keep *me* up at night, and I'm sure it bothered lots of theoretical physicists.

If you are keeping up with things so far, you can probably guess that advances in multidimensional mathematics have enabled the inclusion of both relativity and quantum mechanics at the level of eleven (or more) dimensions. Work is not complete, but it's very well documented. As a result, it is commonly (not universally) accepted that there are multiple dimensions, and the number might be as many as ten, eleven, twenty-six, or more, depending on how you count.

Fans of Terry Pratchett's *Discworld* novels know how trolls count: one, two, many. It works for them. For our purposes, you only need to count: one, two, three, many. Don't fret about what's happening in the ninth dimension; you can only really see one; you imagine two more; and you can get a headache if you try to go for four.

This whole discussion is to open your mind not only to the possibility of more spatial dimensions than the three you are familiar with (height, width, and depth) but also to the fact that the top scientists in the world believe *many additional dimensions exist.*

Visualizing Dimensions

This is something you may have done before, but we are going through the exercise again. The idea is to imagine what happens in *fewer* dimensions so we can put "extra" dimensions into perspective.[8] As we travel in our minds from fewer to more dimensions, we can visualize what happens, observe consistent patterns, and apply those patterns to additional dimensions.

During this discussion, I use the word *consciousness* as existing in an n-dimensional universe instead of describing some sort of critter. Other descriptions of one- or two-dimensional "worlds" and "beings" bother me because their existence doesn't make sense, which is very distracting. Therefore, I use *consciousness,* which is the observer in the n-dimensional universe under discussion. In all cases involving an n-dimensional universe, the universe in question is intended to represent a limited frame of reference, not the universe that describes all of existence.

Branes

As physicists began to explain the universe in terms of many dimensions they needed a convenient way to reference the number of dimensions in which they were working. The solution was to invent a new word—"Brane"—which is based upon the word "membrane," a word that references a two-dimensional surface.

---

[8] There is really no such thing as a one-, two-, or for that matter, three-dimensional universe. I believe that all things exist in all dimensions. The following discussion is for visualization purposes only.

The word "brane" is preceded by the number of dimensions being referenced. A point in space that has no dimension is a 0-brane. You typically think of the universe as three dimensional, which is a 3-brane. If you refer to the passage of time through the universe, that would be a 4-brane, and so on.

In the following discussion and throughout the rest of the book, I'll use the term "n-brane," where n refers to the number of dimensions as appropriate.

Point (Zero Dimensions, or 0-brane)

A point is nowhere, and points are everywhere. I say it is nowhere because there is no height, width, and depth; everywhere, because a point is a place, and there are places everywhere. To a consciousness in a point, there is absolutely nowhere to go, not even on Saturday night. Like the number *zero,* it is nothing, but its presence makes everything else possible. For the sake of simplicity, we will call the zero-dimensional frame of reference a 0-brane.

Line (One Dimension, or 1-brane)

A one-dimensional universe, or 1-brane, is a string of points, each point dimensionally connected to two others. It is easiest to visualize this as a straight line, although there is no particular reason to do so. To a consciousness in a 1-brane, there are only *two* directions to move – forward and back. This consciousness would be aware of only a perfectly straight line, because in this universe, there *is* no dimension other than forward and back, so there is no reference with which to detect any departure from a perfectly straight line *even though the line may wiggle around in more than one dimension.*

For the sake of simplicity then, imagine this frame *is* a perfectly straight line. This 1-brane stretches to infinity in both directions. Therefore, within this 1-brane, there are *an infinite number* of points (0-branes) which are, in essence, zero-dimensional universes; boring universes, but universes nonetheless.

Plane (Two Dimensions, or 2-brane)

Things are starting to become more interesting as we enter the realm of the two-dimensional universe, or 2-brane. A consciousness in this 2-brane can not only move forward and backward, but also side-to-side. This is the world of Donkey Kong!

Unlike the world of Donkey Kong, the "real" 2-brane stretches to infinity in all directions—all directions except up and down, of course, because no such thing exists in a 2-brane.[9] Our consciousness in this 2-brane can see only a perfectly flat plane because there is no reference with which to detect any departure from a perfectly flat plane *even though the plane may wave or crumple in more than two dimensions.*

For the sake of simplicity then, imagine this universe *is* a perfectly flat plane. It stretches to infinity in all horizontal directions. Let's use our 2-brane consciousness to imagine our 1-brane (a perfectly straight line). It is running through the space right next to you, stretching away into infinity in both directions. You cannot see it because it has no width; it is not even as wide as a single atom, and you certainly would not be able to see a string

---

[9] Okay, Donkey Kong has up and down, but he can't move forward or back. Same thing.

of individual atoms. However, it is there, and along this line are an infinite number of points (0-branes).

What is particularly interesting is that this line (1-brane) is passing through points (0-branes) in your 2-brane universe. The point with the incredibly bored 0-brane consciousness is actually a part of two entirely separate universes other than itself! The 0-brane consciousness cannot "see" the 1-brane universe because it has no frame of reference, and the 1-brane consciousness cannot see the 2-brane universe, again, because it lacks a frame of reference (it can only "see" forward and back, not side-to-side).

While you ponder this perfectly straight line (1-brane), imagine there is another perfectly straight-line that runs exactly parallel to the first. In fact, you can imagine that in the space available, there would be room for an infinite number of these 1-branes in your 2-brane universe! Each of the infinite number of 1-branes contains an infinite number of 0-branes (points along the line of the 1-brane).

In fact, now that you think about it, there is no reason whatsoever that the 1-brane universes have to be parallel. They can be running every which way, and it's indeed possible that the 1-branes can intersect one another at any given point. Not only that, but they can intersect at any angle. In our 2-brane world, there are an infinite number of directions, and therefore it is possible for an infinite number of 1-branes to pass through every point in our 2-brane!

Thinking a little bit harder, you realize that not only *can* there be but there *must* be an infinite number of 1-branes intersecting each and every point in my 2-brane universe. I'm not saying that each of these universes is occupied by a consciousness, but because the points (0-branes) exist, the lines (1-branes) also exist.

Whatever is in any given 0-brane is also in every one of the infinite number of *n*-brane universes (where *n*>0) that contains that 0-brane.

Beer Break

Take a few moments to ponder that last bit.

That's a *lot* of universes. For every point that contains something, that specific *something* exists in every universe in which that point exists. For every point (0-brane) inside your body that little bit of stuff that is part of the atom that is part of the molecule that is part of the cell that is part of your body exists exactly as it is in every *n*-brane universe in which that particular 0-brane exists.

Welcome Back to Earth (Three Dimensions)

Have a look around. That's what a consciousness sees in what we will call a three-dimensional universe, or 3-brane. You can see up, down, left and right, forward and back. In our 3-brane universe, we can stack an infinite number of 2-brane universes, each one of which contains an infinite number of 1-branes, each one of which contains an infinite number of 0-branes. A consciousness in the 2-brane (or 1-, or 0-brane) universe can't "see" us because it has no frame of reference with regard to height.

All of these dimensions exist in your world. You can measure them or create a mathematical map to describe any line (straight or curved); plane (flat or bumpy); or the location of any point; and determine whether or not that point falls on any given line or plane. We call that geometry.

Time: The Fourth Dimension

I can help you visualize 0-brane, 1-brane, and 2-brane universes by calling them a point, line, and a plane. You don't need me to visualize a 3-brane universe; you do it on your own all the time.

Time is a bit of a problem, because we can *think* about it, but we can't actually detect it with one of our sensory inputs (eyes, ears, etc.). So time gets a bit tricky to describe with words, even though everybody knows what it is.

What is very interesting is that we already describe time as though it were a fourth dimension. When you meet somebody for coffee, you say, "Let's get together at the coffee shop on the corner of Main and Elm at 2:00." We talk about fictional "time travelers" as moving forward and backward through time. We say *time passes*. We describe time as *passing quickly* or *time slowing down*. We instinctively use spatial coordinates to describe a location in, for lack of a better word, *time*.

Initially, you may dismiss this as a semantic trick we use because we have no sensory reference for time. In other words, if you try to describe something you've never seen before, you tend to use metaphorical language, such as: *the aurora borealis is a shimmering curtain in the sky.* It doesn't work very well, and if you've ever seen a brilliant aurora and tried to describe it, you accentuate this description by looking up at the ceiling, waving your arms and wiggling your fingers (at least *I* do). Maybe we use *place* and *distance* words to describe time because there just isn't anything else to use.

However, the aurora is something relatively few people have experienced, and time is something that *everybody* experiences. You would think we would have specific words for time because, after all, we made up all of the words in our language. Why didn't we make up special words for the passage of time (darn, that's *another* one)?

Well, that's because time is a literal spatial dimension. We may not consciously think of it that way, but it is, in fact, the basis for Einstein's theory of relativity. It is called spacetime.

What My Teachers Never Told Me about Relativity

Criticizing my teachers gives me a bit of heartburn; after all, they must have done a fine job, or I certainly wouldn't be able to write a book. However, I remember studying about relativity[10] in public school. We saw pictures of squashed trains and squashed observers, and a picture of a photon bouncing between two mirrors. We heard stories about the astronaut who traveled to Alpha Centauri at near light-speed, who, upon his return in a few years, finds his twin brother is an old man with grandchildren (or some variation on that story). I went to the library, and I studied a popular science book with a chapter on the subject.

I also remember pretty much all of us kids not understanding a word of it.

I don't know whether I was just too obtuse to understand what I was being taught, or whether the teachers didn't understand what they were teaching and therefore skipped over important information, or the authors who wrote the books simply didn't put it in there. Somehow, though, a *really important* bit of information

---

[10] There are two theories of relativity developed by Einstein: special relativity and general relativity. Special relativity is where he introduced the famous equation, $e=mc^2$. It deals with matter, time, and energy. General relativity accommodates gravity into the equation and deals with the curvature of spacetime and the equivalence of gravity and acceleration. I don't distinguish these in the text, but make reference (in layman's terms) to both.

never made its way into my thick skull. I hate to place the blame on the educational system or my teachers, but somewhere along the line, somebody completely missed the boat on this one. I have asked a lot of people about this, and nobody seems to remember learning about it.

We all learned that Einstein proposed the speed of light was constant (the "*c*" in *e=mc²*). We also learned that time slows down as you approach the speed of light. This is the part where we tend to get lost. This slowing of time is what confused me, especially when it turns out that from the point of view of two observers, time always slows down for the *other* guy. That's just plain ridiculous, although the theory has been proven to be absolutely accurate in experiments.

Here's the part they left out. It's not just light that is traveling at the speed of light. *Everything* is traveling at the speed of light (including you and me). The difference between us and light is that we are traveling in a different direction in one of the dimensions – namely the dimension of *time*.

♦ ♦ ♦ ♦

This is actually fairly easy to understand by drawing an analogy in three dimensions. Imagine two roads in relatively flat terrain. The first road is ten miles long and goes in a straight line from Start to Finish. The second road also begins at Start, but takes the scenic route and curves around through the countryside before it gets to Finish. The second road is twenty miles long because of all the curves.

Imagine two cars and a helicopter, each traveling at exactly sixty miles per hour. One car follows the first road, the other the second road, and the helicopter also follows the second road during its flight. All three begin their trip at the same time starting from the same location (Start) and end at the same location (Finish). For the sake of simplicity, let's eliminate acceleration and braking; they are just moving sixty miles per hour relative to the Start location. Who gets there first, and who gets there last?

The answer is pretty obvious. The car on the first road gets there in ten minutes, the car on the second road gets there in twenty minutes, and the helicopter arrives last. The helicopter not only had to take all twenty miles along the scenic route, it also had to climb into the air and descend to the ground, which took more time, depending on how high it flew over the road. Obviously, for different vehicles traveling at a constant speed, you need to measure the distance traveled in *all three dimensions* in order to predict the correct arrival sequence.

What Einstein so brilliantly pointed out is that everything has a fixed speed in this universe, but *you have to measure distance in all* **four** *dimensions.* Thus, if you have movement in the height, width, and depth dimensions, *time* will slow down proportionally – as with our helicopter, it takes longer to get there from the point of view of somebody waiting at the Finish. The relative part of all of this is that *exactly like the two cars and the helicopter,* everything is moving at exactly the same speed. From the point of view of the helicopter pilot, everything is normal and proceeding at 60 mph. From the standpoint of the observer waiting at Finish, the other two vehicles were obviously faster, even though the observer at Start insists they left at the same time and speed.

In four dimensions, if you are completely at rest in the three spatial dimensions, time passes at the maximum possible rate. As far as you and I are concerned, time stands still on a photon of light because it is using all of its speed traveling in a straight line

(1-brane) through space[11] at hundreds of millions of miles per hour. Meantime, you and I are literally *screaming* through *time* at an unimaginable rate of speed as we sit on our chair finishing the beer we started a couple of pages ago. We are all, according to the theory of relativity, traveling at the same speed. You and I, unlike the photon, are flying in the helicopter along the scenic route, moving through space in three dimensions, plus time.

This concept of a universal constant speed answers a lot of questions, some I have already asked, and a few I have not yet proposed. Because this constant is referred to by Einstein as "*C*" (as in "*mc²*"), I will also do so. For clarity, I'll refer to it as your "*C* quota" because it is an absolute requirement.

Let's Revisit Earth (3-brane) for a Quick Recap

The implications of time as a fourth dimension are simple and profound. When I earlier discussed 0-brane, 1-brane, 2-brane, and 3-brane universes, I intentionally assumed the existence of *time,* or the *4-brane* universe (I'll bet you didn't notice). I did that because you needed the reference of time for visualization. Now, I'm going to ask you to revisit the familiar 3-brane universe, except this time I want you to *really* visualize the 3-brane universe. The universe you visited earlier was actually a 4-brane universe because it included time. So, let's remove time from our visualization.

What happens in our 3-brane universe where time stands still? The answer is "absolutely nothing." Without the dimension of *time*, absolutely nothing changes. Every point is completely

---

[11] Space itself is curved, but that's another discussion. Remember that a 1-brane does not have to be a straight line.

frozen. This is an important concept, and we will return to this later in the book.

More Dimensions

I've mentioned that the existence of more than our four familiar dimensions is widely accepted among physicists, mainly because it simply makes sense out of things that *don't* otherwise make sense. For the rest of this book, you simply have to take my word for this. However, feel free to go get other books and read about it for yourself. If you don't agree with me, go argue with them. I didn't make this up, but it certainly makes sense.

For the purpose of the following descriptions, all references to dimensions will assume the existence of time. I will arbitrarily refer to a frame of reference having fewer dimensions as "lower order universe" and a frame of reference having more dimensions as "higher order universe."

As we review our travels from 0-brane to 1-brane, to 2-brane and finally 3-brane universes, we can make some very consistent observations:

- Every universe exists in an infinite number[12] of higher-order universes.

- Any higher-order universe contains an infinite number of lower-order universes.

---

[12] I use the term "infinite number" rather loosely. The numbers may actually be finite, and the size of the 0-brane is quite likely to be near a Planck Length in diameter, which is *not* infinitely small, although for all intents and purposes, it might as well be. When I say an "infinite number" of something, I'm actually just saying it is a number so large as to be indistinguishable from infinite—"virtually infinite," so to speak.

- Anything that exists in any universe also exists in every higher-order universe to which it also belongs.

- From the point of view of any universe, a consciousness cannot observe anything that exists in a higher-order universe in its entirety.

These are very important deductions, so we'll briefly review each one of them.

• Every Universe Exists in an Infinite Number of Higher-Order Universes

A point (0-brane) is a particular place. Any 1-brane, 2-brane, 3-brane, or higher-order universe containing that place contains the original 0-brane. An infinite number of lines or planes may pass through a particular point, an infinite number of planes may pass through a line, and so on. Therefore, each universe exists in an infinite number of higher-order universes.

• Any Higher-Order Universe Contains an Infinite Number of Lower-Order Universes

This is the inverse of the preceding statement. Our 3-brane universe contains an infinite number of planes, lines, and points, and each plane contains an infinite number of lines, and so on. Therefore, each non-zero-dimensional universe contains an infinite number of lower-order universes.

• Anything that Exists in any Universe also Exists in Every Higher-Order Universe to which It also Belongs

This is fairly self-explanatory, but I am stating it as a given circumstance. In a 0-brane, if there is a piece of "stuff," that particular piece of stuff will be part of the higher-order universes in which it is located.

If we were to use your body as an example, we can describe any number of points within your body, lines passing through your body, or planes bisecting your body. We can pick a point in your heart, a point that happens to represent a universe containing a fundamental building block (perhaps a quark) of an atom surrounding that point.

If we spear a line through the same point, the 0-brane represented by the point is part of the line and contains the same building block for that particular atom. As we move along the line, it passes through an infinite number of 0-branes. Along the line and close to the first point there may be additional building blocks for that particular atom (or not)[13]. The line (a 1-brane) may pass through other atoms, and some of those points along the line might contain the building blocks for those atoms that compose your spine, skin, blood, and so on.

If we then describe a plane (a 2-brane universe) across the previously described 1-brane, all of the above building blocks would be there, plus all additional points to the left and right of the original line. It would represent a "slice" of your body and all of the component building blocks that happen to fall along the slice.

Notice that there would be no actual atoms in the slice, because the 2-brane universe represented by the slice is only 0-brane thick; there is no thickness. Even though it is very tiny, an

---

[13] There's actually more space than stuff in an atom. Much like a rock traveling through interstellar space could travel right through our solar system and never hit anything, a line or plane can intersect an atom without encountering any particles at all. In fact, more often than not, that will be exactly the case.

atom actually has a thickness. Therefore, only the building blocks of atoms would exist in the 2-brane universe.[14]

When we add the third dimension, we now add layer upon layer of 2-brane universes, including all the 1-brane and 0-branes they contain. As we stack the building blocks, they build atoms, molecules, cells, organs, blood, bone, and eventually your whole body. If we add the fourth dimension—time—you will now be able to breathe.

Pretty exciting, huh?

- **From the Point of View of any Universe, a Consciousness Cannot Observe Anything in Its Entirety that Exists in a Higher-Order Universe**

If I am observing you from the 2-brane universe described above, I will be able to see the occasional pieces of "stuff" from which the atoms are made that make up your body. My universe is zero-dimensions thick, so I am unable to observe even those atoms, just the pieces of the atoms. There is no possibility I could observe your entire body.

◆ ◆ ◆ ◆

As we make these consistent assumptions, we can project the same assumptions with regard to observing the fifth and higher dimensions from our four-dimensional perspective; namely, that we can't see squat in the fifth dimension. Let's not even bother talking about eleven. Seriously.

---

[14] In the current view of superstring theory, which includes the existence of multiple dimensions, a vibrating string loop is the "something" that is the fundamental building block of everything. The substance of every string is exactly the same; the only difference is the manner in which the string vibrates. This determines its energy, which determines its properties, and determines exactly what building block it is.

However, just as physicists can explain certain otherwise inexplicable behaviors using additional dimensions, we can do the same.

Recap

- Success Principles are about increasing your odds of success. Used properly, the odds of success increase to the point that it seems like magic.

- The macroscopic universe is huge; it is enormous beyond our capacity to imagine.

- The microscopic universe is tiny; the cells, atoms, and subatomic particles that exist are so numerous and so small it is also beyond our capacity to imagine.

- A dimension is not a place; it is a direction.

- More than one hundred years ago, Einstein proposed first four, then five dimensions in special and general relativity theories. Modern string theory proposes many more. The existence of more than three dimensions that we can perceive is a generally accepted principle of physics.

- You only need to count dimensions like a troll: one, two, three, many.

- Consistent observations about dimensions are:

  ➢ Every universe exists in an infinite number of higher-order universes.

  ➢ Any higher-order universe contains an infinite number of lower-order universes.

  ➢ Anything that exists in any universe also exists in every higher-order universe to which it also belongs.

  ➢ From the point of view of any universe, a consciousness cannot observe anything in its entirety that exists in a higher-order universe

12

The Results

In chapter 4, I had you perform a simple exercise, namely, raising one or both hands (or not). Perhaps you forgot, but I didn't. If you wish, you can do it again (or not). Here's the point of the exercise.

You consciously decided what to do. Even choosing to do nothing was a conscious choice. There were four possibilities: do nothing, raise your left hand, your right hand, or both hands. You decided what to do. You might have even changed your mind, but that doesn't matter. You did *something*, even if all you did was think about it and decided to do nothing.

♦ ♦ ♦ ♦

Let's consider the physical process of thinking. In this case, I'm not talking about the intangible consciousness we cannot see, but the *results* of conscious thinking that can be measured with devices such as an electroencephalograph (EEG) or functional magnetic resonance imaging (fMRI). Using computer modeling, we can build a simulated moving picture of the brain activity that takes place when we think or visualize something. Where there is brain activity, the area of the brain lights up; the more activity, the more lights.

What we are actually seeing is the electrical activity created when a tiny amount of chemical (called a neurotransmitter) is released by a brain cell (neuron) where it joins another brain cell. This causes an electrochemical reaction that stimulates the adjacent brain cell, and this electrochemical reaction is what we measure. When there is a lot of light on our simulated model of the brain, it means a lot of neurons are zapping each other with neurotransmitters in the lighted area.[1]

All of this activity happens when we think. We have roughly twenty billion or so neurons in our brain. In terms of modern computers, that doesn't seem like a whole lot (three gigabytes), except for one thing—neurons don't have a single pair of connections to a linear bus. They can have a lot of connections, and the connections are networked. In fact, the typical neuron has over *seven thousand active dendritic connections* to other neurons in an extraordinary neural web of hundreds of *trillions* of connections.

Amazing as that is, it's not really the point. The point is the incredibly complex activity happening at the cellular level is multiplied trillions of times yet again at the atomic level! Every thought involves millions of neurons; each little squirt of neural happy juice is made of billions of molecules composed of atoms that are, in turn, composed of subatomic building blocks. When you did *nothing*, you still actually caused trillions of subatomic reactions to occur in your brain. If you did raise a hand, your decision caused trillions of additional minute chemical reactions to occur in your brain and nervous system, which in turn caused the billions of cells in a couple of dozen muscles to contract or relax in such a way that your hand or hands moved in accordance

---

[1] The electroencephalograph infers neural activity by measuring electrical activity on the scalp. fMRI measures blood flow associated with neural activity directly.

with your thought. Furthermore, if you *did* raise your hand, your hand and arm are actually quite heavy. Your brain is processing input from all over your body, including your eyes and inner ears, and will notice that you may be heading to an off-balance state as your hand moves. Your brain then is *also* constantly responding to this stimuli with minute changes to your supporting core muscles. The result is that you can raise your hand without falling over.

♦ ♦ ♦ ♦

The two main points to note are:

1. You made a conscious choice.

2. Your conscious choice initiated an unimaginable number of events at the microscopic level.

Most people, when they choose to do something "simple," like raising a hand or lifting a finger, see only the hand or finger being raised and count it as a single event. In actuality, the hand going up into the air is the *result* of trillions of events at the macro- and microscopic levels. Cells contract, neurons fire, chemicals are synthesized and released, minute electrical signals are transmitted, and tiny nuclear reactions occur at the subatomic scale. Not only that, your body and brain and associated sensory input feel a weight shift and make similar adjustments to redistribute your body weight, and your eyes and ears continue to receive the sensory input (watching your hand rise or making sure it didn't) after which time the brain stores the information away. It's fairly safe to say you had no idea all that stuff was happening, but it was. Just ask any doctor.

Here's the question. *Why did all of that stuff happen?* It happened because your consciousness (the one we *can't* measure) visualized a hand going up and sent the command, "Make it so!"

♦ ♦ ♦ ♦

Imagine you are an alien watching the Starship Enterprise, and suddenly there was a flurry of activity, the crew suddenly got busy, lights started blinking, the machinery wound up, and then it just warped off into space and vanished. You look at your alien comrade and ask, "Why the hell did it do *that?*"

What you didn't see was that the Enterprise sensors detected your presence, and the first officer advised the captain (Piccard in this example) it might be best to beat a hasty retreat to a safe distance on vector 297 at warp factor 2, and Captain Piccard said, "Make it so!"

Imagine you read chapter 4 at the local coffee shop, put the book down, raised both hands in the air, and then picked up the book again. Somebody noticed, looked at the person nearby, and asked, "Why on earth did that person do that?"

You get the idea. There's something going on in there that you can't see. Even with our amazing brains, they simply don't have the capacity to set such an enormous number of processes in motion, much less deal with the phenomenal complexity of everything that is going on, any more than Jean-Luc Piccard can make the Starship Enterprise attain warp speed all by himself with nothing but a paddle and lots of willpower.

♦ ♦ ♦ ♦

Did the brain activity (the part we can measure) cause you to think? Or did thinking cause the brain activity? It's the old chicken-and-egg question, and it has the same simple answer.

The egg didn't lay itself, and it didn't appear out of thin air. The chicken came first. Maybe not the exact brand of chicken we have today, but some sort of chicken-like critter laid the first egg. If you are a modern farmer breeding a new chicken, some sort of chicken has to lay the first egg that hatches the new breed.

If the thoughts we have are simply the byproduct of trillions of random subatomic reactions, then considering all of the thoughts happening in billions and billions of brains all across the earth (my cat has thoughts, too, every time he sees a grocery bag), to assume that all of these billions and billions of trillions of random subatomic events happen to end up producing coherent thought in these billions of brains--well, I'd have to say it was a lot more likely that a fully developed, modern-day chicken egg just popped out of a volcano and hatched the ancestor to all chickens everywhere.

Just like the Starship Enterprise didn't just warp out of space for no reason, and just like your hands didn't pop into the air because of some random chemical reaction, there was a motive force behind the activity. The thought came first.

♦ ♦ ♦ ♦

This now puts us squarely in the dilemma of trying to figure out what "consciousness" is, because it is this immeasurable consciousness that's causing all of these creative thoughts that are causing all of this activity. One of the first things you do in trying to identify something is to *find* it. Where is the consciousness?

As I mentioned earlier, nobody has found it. All we see are the traces it leaves behind as brainwave patterns on the equipment with which we measure these things. In addition, we see traces of it in the activity throughout our body. We see manifestations of consciousness in all kinds of animals, even insects that have very different brain structures than humans. If you stop and think about it, as the fictional Starship Enterprise accelerates to warp speed and vanishes, you are seeing a manifestation of Captain Jean-Luc Piccard's consciousness as he commanded the ship.

Manifestations of consciousness are all over the place, and yet consciousness itself nowhere to be found.

I'm hoping at this point that you are connecting the dots. What else have we discussed that exists and cannot be measured? Something there that we can't see?

Well, for an observer, pretty much anything that exists in a universe having more dimensions than the reference universe of the observer exhibits those characteristics. Remember this deduction?

- *From the point of view of any universe, a consciousness cannot observe anything in its entirety that exists in a higher-order universe.*

If that's the case, then our consciousness shows every sign of existing as *something* in a fifth (or higher) dimension. This is exactly what we expect, because our entire bodies also exist in the additional dimensions (*anything that exists in any universe also exists in every higher-order universe to which it belongs*), but we simply don't have the correct sensory apparatus to detect what's happening in those additional dimensions.

Wow. That's a mouthful. Before you spit it out, I'd like to remind you that you are *already* aware of existing in a dimension you can't sense – namely, the dimension of time.

◆ ◆ ◆ ◆

Hopefully, you have been led willingly down the path to this concept – namely, that you exist as a being in more than three, and even more than four dimensions, and that your consciousness (which nobody has really been able to locate) might reside somewhere you are unable to see, or even imagine. Let's review:

- We know and can measure three dimensions using only our bodies.

- We are aware of the existence of time as a fourth dimension by the observation of change; we use instruments to measure the passage and effects of time.

- Physicists today are exploring the probability of all matter and energy in our universe as belonging to ten, eleven, or more dimensions (one of which is time).[2]

If you accept the existence of more than three spatial dimensions (and there are profound reasons to do so, both mathematically and logically), then you must also accept that all matter as you know it exists in all of those dimensions. You are made of matter, and that means that you are a ten, eleven, twenty-six, or whatever-number-dimensional being, whether you realize it or not. Just because you see a thing doesn't mean you see *every*

---

[2] Superstring theory has been described as being "…so ambitious that it can only be totally right, or totally wrong." The primary hurdle in general acceptance is the extreme difficulty in experimental verification. Normally, physicists observe phenomena and construct theories to explain the observations. Those theories are subject to rigorous testing and confirmation. In the case of superstring theory, we have a mathematically elegant theory that accommodates observed phenomena but predicts *additional* phenomena yet to be observed. Like many others, I have found the concept of multiple dimensions to be very appealing in that it can be used to explain many otherwise inexplicable events in a consistent way. However, because of the difficulty of creating experiments to measure the new phenomena, this rigorous testing and confirmation has yet to be done.

part of it. That applies to yourself as well as other things. Remember these other deductions?

- Every universe exists in an infinite number of higher-order universes.

- Any higher-order universe contains an infinite number of lower-order universes.

- Anything that exists in any universe also exists in every higher-order universe that it also belongs to.

To rephrase: every part of yourself you see and measure exists in one or more dimensions that you are unaware of. If you recall our definition of "awareness," the *reason* you are unaware of these dimensions is because you do not have the sensory apparatus to detect them.

Because you do not have the necessary sensory apparatus, you do not even have a reference to use to *imagine* what exists in those additional dimensions. Thus, you have no way to truly visualize your entire self, any more than you can envision your three-dimensional body by looking at the scattered subatomic "stuff" that exists in a two-dimensional slice through your body.

Because our consciousness is not something we can see or measure (we can only observe the *results* of our consciousness), it is—to use the words of our friend Bomb #20—*intuitively obvious* that a significant part of our consciousness functions in dimensions beyond the three we can directly observe.

If matter exists in more than four dimensions, and you are made of matter, then you exist in more than four dimensions. If your consciousness is part of you, then your consciousness also exists in more than four dimensions. At any given time, your sensory apparatus is *aware* of only one dimension.[3] It is through this very limited sensory apparatus that we gather the information from which we construct *all* of our beliefs. As a consequence, our understanding of the universe around us is incomplete at best; more likely, it is completely wrong. For instance, it is obvious from our senses that Earth is standing still and everything in the sky is moving. It would be silly to think that we are actually traveling the better part of one thousand miles per hour on the surface of a ball spinning in space, right? Wouldn't we feel that?

We know Earth is spinning and that the surface of Earth is spinning more than one thousand miles per hour relative to its axis[4], and we know Earth orbits the sun. As a race, our knowledge

---

[3] For instance, the retina of each of our eyes has about 130 million cells, and each can detect a single photon. These photons are traveling in one dimension, so each cell is able to sense in a single dimension. The brain aggregates and interprets the hundreds of millions of one-dimensional bits of information to form a two-dimensional view, and then uses the separate information from each of your two eyes to infer a third dimension. When we touch something, we touch only the surface, and in fact only "feel" each nerve ending. Our brain interprets the many nerve inputs to infer a two-dimensional construct. We need to combine multiple inputs to construct a three-dimensional "reality" within our brain (we reach around the object to see how thick it is). In a similar fashion, we observe changes in our sensory input to infer the passage of time. Thus, we *think* we are observing four dimensions (including time), but in reality, we sense only one dimension from hundreds of millions of different sources simultaneously.

[4] At the equator: the radius of Earth averages approximately 3959 miles, and circumference is calculated as $2\pi R$. Thus, Earth is about 24,875 miles in circumference, and revolves once every 24 hours. Your actual speed relative to the axis of rotation is closer to 800 mph if you are in the United States or Europe. If you want to toss in the rotation of Earth around the sun, add another 66,000 mph or so.

and sophistication is growing. Just as our brain can take a pair of two-dimensional images, one from each of our eyes, and visualize a third dimension (depth), we can also visualize Earth turning on its axis, while it, in turn, revolves around the sun, even though we have no direct experience of those phenomena.

In the following chapters, you will be introduced to things that have a profound effect on the course of your life but that you cannot directly observe. These concepts revolve around those parts of you (including your consciousness) that exist but that you cannot see.

Recap

- The events that we measure in the brain represent the *results* of conscious thought, not thought itself.

- We can observe the results of conscious thought (such as raising a hand, or specific brain activity) without being able to directly observe the consciousness initiating the action.

- Scientists have measured in five dimensions and believe that there are more. Matter, simply by existing, exists in all dimensions, however many that happens to be.

- We are made of matter, and therefore we exist in more than the three dimensions that we believe we can see.

- Our sensory apparatus is able to sense in a single dimension. Our brain aggregates hundreds of millions of inputs from our sensory apparatus to build a two- or three- dimensional construct in our mind. We are not able to perceive in more than one dimension; we only *think* we can.

- Consciousness is something that we have been unable to measure directly. We exist in more dimensions than we are able to observe, so the existence of something about ourselves that we are unable to observe or measure is likely to be operating in those dimensions that are beyond our ability to sense.

13

Travel

Einstein's Happy Thought

After his success with the theory of relativity, Albert Einstein turned his mind to the challenge of incorporating gravity into the theory. At some point, he realized that gravity is indistinguishable from acceleration and later stated this was the happiest thought of his life. This realization allowed him to develop the general theory of relativity, and the predictions made with his theory later confirmed the validity of his calculations.

I had a very similar thought. I can't say it was the happiest thought of my life, but it did make me jump out of my chair and shout!

Keep Your Eye on the Ball

A ball, or sphere, is a three dimensional object. No matter how you slice a sphere with a two-dimensional plane, you end up with a circle. If we were to place our point of view in a two-dimensional universe, and then pass a sphere through our universe, we would see a point, followed by an enlarging line. After it reached the maximum circumference, the line would then get progressively smaller until it became a point and then vanished (Figure 13-1).

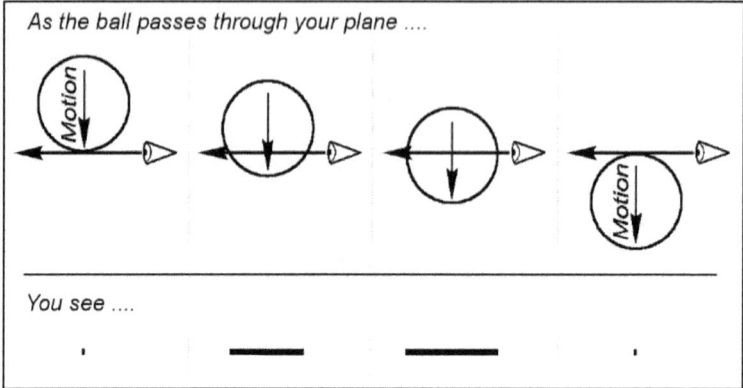

Figure 13- 1. *A sphere passing through a plane.*

That's the case with the observer (you) at rest in a universe (2-brane in this case) and an object from a higher-order universe (3-brane) moving through your two-dimensional universe. Remember, an observer in a two dimensional universe can't see an entire three-dimensional object, but he *can* see the parts of it that move through his universe.

What if instead of moving the sphere, the sphere was at rest and we moved the *observer* (you) through the adjacent planes (2-brane universes) occupied by the sphere (Figure 13-2)?

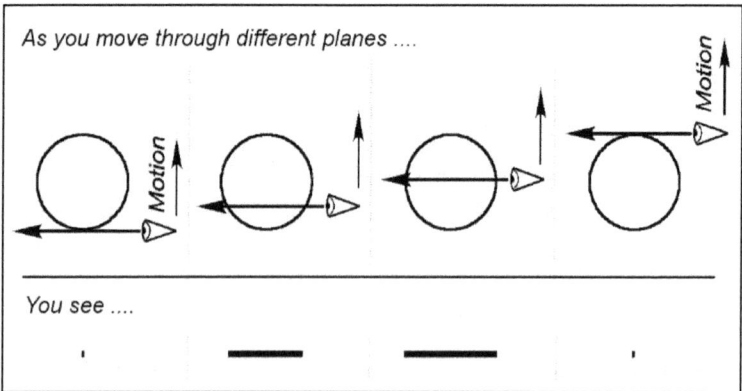

Figure 13- 2. *Moving the observer past a sphere at rest.*

Would you be able to tell the difference? The answer is, "No, you would see no difference between (a) moving the sphere through one 2-brane universe that you occupy, or (b) moving you through adjacent 2-brane universes past the sphere."

Let's take a look using an experiment we can construct. We can't actually put ourselves in a 2-brane universe, but we can simulate being in one. Let's mount a video camera in a box that has a narrow horizontal slit, as in Figure 13-3. This will represent

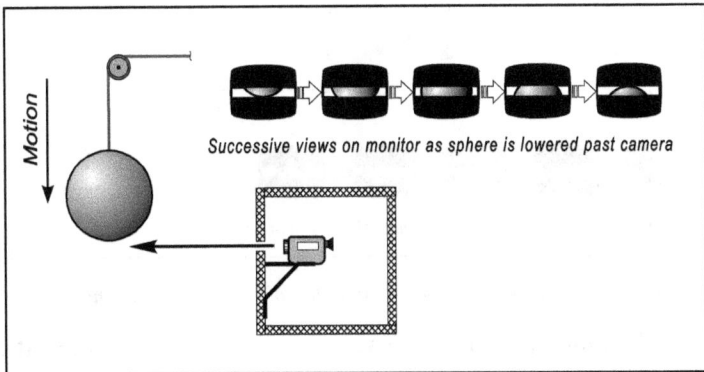

Successive views on monitor as sphere is lowered past camera

Figure 13- 3. *An experiment simulating a two-dimensional viewpoint.*

our two-dimensional point of view.[1] If we lower a ball on a string past the slit, we will see a fine point expand to the diameter of the ball and then reduce back to a point. We'll see the string as the ball is lowered past the slit, but that's the price of the experiment. The object is to simulate the point of view of a two-dimensional

---

[1] A very interesting phenomenon is that any observer in an *n*-dimensional universe can only observe *n*-1 dimensions. A one-dimensional observer looking along the line in either direction can only see a point. A two-dimensional observer can only see a line (represented here by the slit). We, in three dimensions, can only see a plane. Our stereoscopic vision is simply combining two two-dimensional views (one from each eye) to imagine a third dimension within our consciousness.

observer. When we play back the recording on a screen, the view will be similar to the view of the two-dimensional observer described earlier.

What if *both* the box with the video camera and the ball were suspended as shown in Figure 13-4?

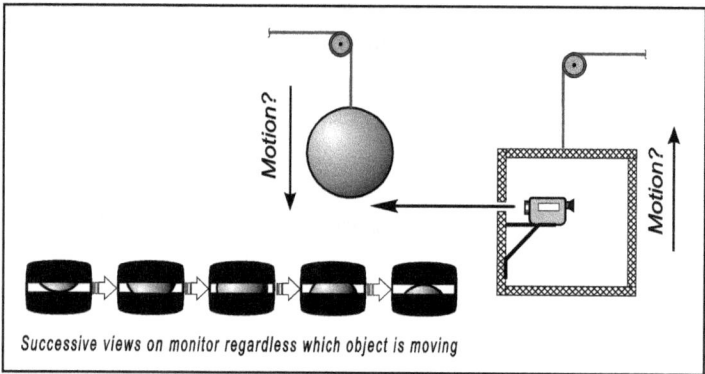

Successive views on monitor regardless which object is moving

Figure 13- 4. *The experiment where both the sphere and box can move.*

By looking at a video replay, would you be able to tell if I lowered the ball or raised the camera? Suppose I were feeling frisky that day and moved both the camera *and* the ball in opposite directions? Would you be able to tell?

The answer is you would have no idea whether I moved the *ball* through the cameras field of view or if the ball was at rest and I moved the camera. All you would be able to determine is that something changed, and that change would be the same whether the point of view moved, or the object moved, or both.

Another way of looking at this is that the results are the same if an observer (you) are sitting still in a single universe (or *n*-brane) and something of a higher order (>*n*-brane) passed through, or the thing was at rest and *you* were the one moving through many lower-ordered (*n*-brane) universes.

My **Happy Thought**

If you are still with me on this, you have at least decided not to completely spit out the concept that you are a being that exists in a universe with dimensions you can't see. *In particular*, you have a consciousness that very likely operates, at least in part, outside of the familiar three dimensions.

If you recall from our exercise, your consciousness can set in motion trillions of events from the macroscopic (raising your hand) to the microscopic (billions of neurons firing) to the subatomic (trillions of electrochemical reactions in the space between neurons). That would lead one to think there is more to your consciousness than we normally give credit.

Keep in mind also that Einstein, in his theory of relativity, stated that all mass is in motion, and the sum of the motion among all dimensions is equal to a constant C, or what we know as the speed of light. If we could attain the speed of light (we can't because we exist in three dimensions) time would slow to a stop for us.

Now add to all of this a key ingredient: *you are not able to tell the difference between observing change in a single three-dimensional universe (3-brane) and observing many* different *three-dimensional universes as you move through time. This is the 4-brane universe we observe every day as described in the theory of relativity, and earlier in chapter 11.*

♦ ♦ ♦ ♦

What if part of the universal constant is not just moving through three dimensions plus time? What if traveling through *different* 3-brane universes is what is really happening?

♦ ♦ ♦ ♦

We can easily visualize moving along a line (one dimension) or moving around on a plane (two dimensions), and we not only visualize but actually do move through three dimensions all the time—every time our heart pumps, we take a breath, or (dare I say it?) raise a hand. When we move in three dimensions, forward and backward, left and right, up and down, or any combination, we are traversing uncounted numbers of zero-, one-, and two-dimensional "universes" and scarcely give it a thought.

If we accept that, and also the premise that there are more than three spatial dimensions, doesn't it make sense that we, as four or more dimensional beings, are *also* moving among uncounted numbers of *three*-dimensional universes as well? What we assume is a single universe undergoing constant change might actually be our conscious point of view moving through *different* universes. We are observing the differences between those different universes, just as we observe the change in scenery as we drive along a road in our automobiles, looking out the window.

That is *my* happy thought!

Recap

- An observer in an n-dimensional universe watching an object of greater than n dimensions cannot determine if the object, the observer, or both are moving.

- Humans have the ability to assemble enough information to perceive changes in a three-dimensional universe. Given that time has been determined to be a spatial dimension (spacetime), and that there are more than three dimensions, we cannot determine whether we are in a single universe that is constantly changing, or if we are traveling through many successive, multidimensional universes, and the changes we observe as time are the differences between the universes.

14

Time

This, then, requires some reinterpretation of our concept of time itself. Just as the view changes as we move forward or to the side, if we moved a specific distance in a specific direction in a *fourth* spatial dimension, we would also see differences. Think in terms of moving the camera in Figure 13-4; we are looking in the same direction but seeing a different slice of the ball, so to speak.

If you stop to think about what we "see" when we say that time is passing, you will realize the only thing we use to determine the passage of time is *change*. Even in a dark room, we breathe, our hearts beat. Something is always changing somewhere, and we define this change as the passage of time.

Speed

Think about how fast a photon of light travels—literally at the speed of light, and it travels at that speed in one direction (i.e., dimension). According to our best theories, backed by observation, time stands still for the photon; it is using its entire C-quota moving through one dimension and has no speed left over to move through any other dimension, including the dimension of time.

Think now about yourself. Although we are always moving (Earth is spinning, revolving around the sun, the sun itself is moving, and the Milky Way galaxy is also moving), in comparison to the C quota, we are not traveling through *space* very fast at all. Therefore, according to relativity theory, we are moving through *time* at a velocity approaching the speed of a photon traveling through space. I say "approaching" because, unlike a photon, we exist in more than one dimension and thus have relative motion through those dimensions. We cannot exceed our C quota, so our travel through time must be somewhat slower than C.

Instead of moving through this vague concept of "time," think instead of moving through many static, three-dimensional universes (or 3-branes); universes as densely packed in four dimensions as two- or one-dimensional universes are packed in our familiar three-dimensional universe. Think of everything happening right now as you read this, down to the subatomic level—every heartbeat, every neuron firing, every atom being torn apart in the nuclear fire of every star. There's a lot of stuff happening.

Remember the true three-dimensional universe (3-brane)? Without time, the universe is static; nothing changes at all. If we assume *each* 3-brane is timeless, and consider any change we observe – down to the subatomic level—as an indication that we have traveled from one to another 3-brane (universe), then considering how quickly things are changing, we must be moving unfathomably fast. In fact, we are traveling at nearly the speed of light, and that is why we see such rapid change. That is our intrinsic velocity as defined in the theory of relativity.

♦ ♦ ♦ ♦

Let's pause for a moment and review. Your first question is probably something like, "Golly, wouldn't I *feel* it if I were traveling millions of miles per hour?"

Actually, you wouldn't (and you don't). What you *feel* is acceleration, and you were born going this fast. You know (intellectually, anyway) that you are on the surface of a ball (Earth) spinning in space, and the surface of Earth is moving close to 1,000 miles per hour, and you don't feel that. Earth, itself is orbiting the sun at a speed in excess of 66,000 miles per hour[1], and you don't feel that, either. Not only that, but you are slowing down and speeding up as Earth spins around its *own* axis as well as revolving around the sun, so you are actually accelerating from 65K mph to 67K mph and back every day. You'd *think* you would notice an acceleration of 2,000 miles per hour every day, but you don't feel *that*, either.

Your next question might be, "Wouldn't I *see* it?"

And the answer to that question is the whole point. If you are cruising down the road in a car, how do you know it's moving? You look out the window and see things passing by. A plane? You look out the window and see things move. Earth? You look in the sky and see the stars move in a circle. You see the sun rise and set. We see the background of the stars behind the sun change throughout the year and thus know that Earth (with you on it) is circling the sun.

We know we are moving because we see change every second of every minute of every day. Based on our observation of how quickly things change, we realize we must be moving *very* fast.

---

[1] *Very* approximately, we are 93 million miles from the sun, so Earth travels ~584 million miles per year ($2\pi R$), divided by 365.25 days, divided by 24 hours, equals 66,621 miles per hour.

♦ ♦ ♦ ♦

To examine this further, let's review our high school science and imagine what would happen if we accelerate in one direction and approach the speed of light. We know that time from your point of view remains normal, but compared to an observer at rest, your time slows down; this is in accordance with the theory of relativity and verified with experimental data. Imagine you are observing a far distant pulsar[2], pulsing once every second as seen from Earth. If you board a spaceship and accelerate relative to Earth and the distant pulsar, the blinking of the pulsar would appear to slow down compared to your clock on board the spaceship. Back on Earth, the pulsar would continue to pulse exactly once every second. Time appears to slow down for you as you accelerate, and if you ever *could* reach the speed of light (you can't, but you need to go read up on your Einstein for that explanation), time would completely stop for you. *You would be in a single, timeless, three-dimensional universe (3-brane) where nothing ever changed.* You would be using all of your C-quota to travel along one dimension at the speed of light.

♦ ♦ ♦ ♦

When we mathematically represent two dimensions on a graph, we use x and y for the forward/back and left/right coordinates, and z to represent the up/down coordinates. These

---

[2] After a giant star explodes (supernova), the remaining, compressed core is a neutron star containing enormous amounts of energy. The energy, in the form of electromagnetic radiation, may be focused into a beam by the magnetic field of the neutron star. As the star rotates, this beam sweeps across the universe. As the beam passes Earth every rotation, we see this as a flash, or pulse. We have named these spinning neutron stars *pulsars.*

letters were obviously chosen without regard for the existence of more than three dimensions. When we add a fourth spatial dimension, we throw the whole alphabet in reverse and use the letter *w* for that dimension. It's not higher mathematics; you can do this in a regular off-the-shelf computer spreadsheet. Charles Hinton was a nineteenth century British mathematician who was quite famous for his writings on a fourth spatial dimension, and he coined the terms "ana" and "kata" for directions along the *w* vector.[3]

I am proposing that as you accelerate in the three familiar spatial dimensions, you trade off some of your *C* quota in your travel through three-dimensional universes. If traveling along the *x*, *y*, and *z* axes means we are traveling through zero-, one-, and two-dimensional universes, then traveling along the *x*, *y*, *z*, and *w* axes means we are traveling through zero-, one-, two-, *and three-dimensional* universes.

We know time speeds up and slows down for an observer just as easily (*exactly* as easily) as the observer's velocity through space. In our example above, as we accelerate in the *x*, *y*, and/or *z* vectors, we *decelerate* in the *w* vector. On a two-dimensional graph sheet, using the vertical axis as a reference vector for velocity, when we add vectors of the same length (speed) but change direction (add a horizontal component), even though our

---

[3] This is a brilliant bit of marketing from Mr. Hinton's standpoint. The words are loosely translated Greek for "up" and "down," but "ana" and "kata" sound so much better. It brings to mind the Maserati Quattroporte, or the Ferrari Testa Rossa. Nobody would ever call a luxury sedan the Chevy Fourdoor, or a high-performance sports car the Ford Redhead. Somehow, things sound sexier when translated into some Mediterranean language.

speed (length along the vectors) is constant, our speed *relative to the reference axis* appears to decrease as we increase the

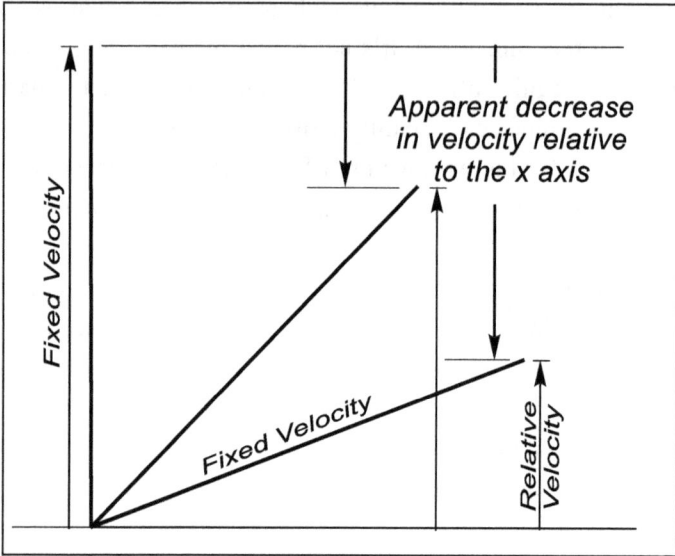

Figure 14- 1. *Velocity relative to a particular direction decreases the further we depart from that direction.*

horizontal deflection (Figure 14-1).

In our spaceship, although the surrounding universe appears to slow down (the pulsar takes more than a second to blink), time to us seems the same (our onboard clock *seems* to tick at the same speed). Using very precise clocks, this is exactly how scientists measure time dilation.

What is actually happening is that Earth, the spaceship, and the pulsar are *all three traveling at velocity C all of the time in all dimensions (directions)*. When we "accelerate" the spaceship, what we are *actually* doing is changing the *vector* of the spaceship. The actual *speed* stays the same. According to the theory of relativity, speed is constant. The velocity of the spaceship (and everything else) is *already C*, and its total speed in all dimensions cannot exceed that. So, in order to accelerate in the *x*, *y* and *z* dimensions, it must decelerate in the *w* dimension in order to maintain *C*. From the point of view on the *spaceship*, the pulsar appears to slow down, but what we actually observe is the pulsar traveling in a different *w* vector than the spaceship, so it *seems* to be moving slower. Let's look at Figure 14-2.

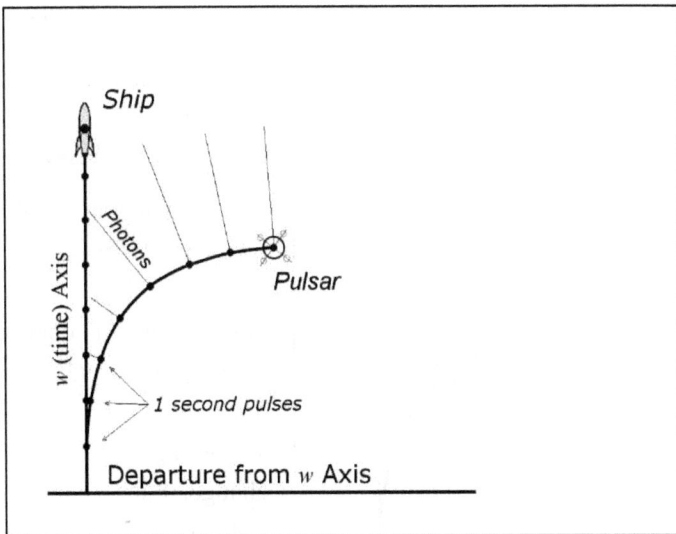

Figure 14- 2. *What appears to be happening from the point of view of the spaceship.*

Both the pulsar and the spaceship are traveling at the same velocity. The length of the line is the same, and the dots represent the passage of one second. This is the same as saying the same amount of time has passed for the symbols at the end of the lines. As the spaceship travels along an axis (*w*), the pulsar falls farther behind *relative to that axis,* and the perceived decrease in relative speed becomes more pronounced as the vector departs further.

Notice that only five photons from the pulsar reach the spaceship, even though eight seconds have passed.

In reality, what is actually happening is more like Figure 14-3. The acceleration of the spaceship is actually changing the *w* vector of the *spaceship*. To somebody on the spaceship, everything looks normal, but everything else is slowing down. At the pulsar, everything looks normal, but time on the spaceship is slowing down. That's the "relativity" part of the theory of relativity. It all depends on your point of view.[4]

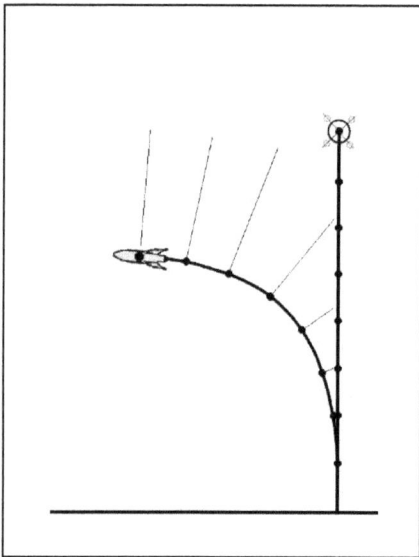

Figure 14- 3

An Odd Conclusion

The conclusion is that time might be nothing more than our observation of change. As we rip through the *w* dimension, we see a staggering amount of change. Each change of state for the elementary particles in our universe counts; an unimaginable number of events happening in the span of a single second of time.

---

[4] Note that because they have only two dimensions, these drawings are very simplistic. In the real universe there are two more dimensions to consider, as well as things like Doppler Effect, which are not considered here.

This alternate view of the universe means that each state change represents a different static 3-brane universe, and we traverse an unimaginable number of these *universes* in the span of what *appears to be* a single second of time. It is exactly as though we are traveling across these universes at speeds approaching the speed of light.

Why does that sound familiar? Stay with me here; this actually does have something to do with you.

Inertia

One last physical phenomenon to discuss is the physical property of inertia. *Inertia* is the resistance of mass to a change in motion. If you have ever tried to push a car, you have hands-on experience with inertia. Once you got it rolling, if you then tried to stop it by pulling, you then gained even more experience, and perhaps a deep respect for your brakes.

The concept of inertia is very important because it applies to *your* motion through the *w* vector as well as the *x, y,* and *z* vectors. The kinetic energy of a body of mass increases with speed. If you pushed your car, it is moving very slowly. You can get around in front of it and push back, and it will *gradually* slow down and stop (provided you didn't push it downhill!). If the car happens to be moving even 10 mph, I suggest you don't get in front of it. Even though you think it's moving slowly, it will just roll right over you. If the car is going at highway speeds and you get in front of it, you simply go *splat!*

What is important to understand here is that you are traveling at the speed of light. You have a *lot* of inertia.

Which means, *you can't just change direction on a dime.*

Recap

- In the absence of time, the universe is absolutely static; nothing changes.

- As we move from one three-dimensional universe (3-brane) to the next, the changes we see are the differences between the universes. We interpret this change as time.

- We are traveling at C, which is tremendously fast. Most of our velocity is along the w axis, which represents the dimension of time. We are moving through time at nearly the speed of light, which explains why we see such an enormous amount of change; we are moving through an enormous number of adjacent 3-branes (three-dimensional universes).

- Time as a dimension (direction) explains the phenomena of time dilation. It is really just an exercise in geometry when plotted against the x, y, and z vectors.

15

A New Way of Looking at Your World

It's time to pull all of this together: consciousness, casting spells, physics, life, the universe, and all that jazz. If I've done my job, you have a whole lot of questions. They aren't all going to be answered in these pages, but I'll at least try to deliver what you signed up for. First, let's take a refresher on what we've read.

Review

We've covered a lot of ground so far. The topics we've covered are:

- Miracles
- An Exercise
- You as the Center of the Universe
- Magic
- Accountability
- Awareness and Consciousness
- Crafting and Casting Spells
- Psychology
- Physics

Here's a brief review of each topic:

You are surrounded by "**Miracles**" and miraculous events, from the entire cosmos to your mobile phone.

You are "**The Center of the Universe**" you live in. Every bit of knowledge and experience you have was obtained through your senses.

You performed "**An Exercise**" in which you caused trillions upon trillions of events to occur.

You learned that *any sufficiently advanced technology is indistinguishable from* "**Magic.**" We learned from the story of Harry Potter that with magic, as with technology, you must still factor in the "magic" of others whose universe overlaps yours.

"**Accountability**" means There Ain't No Such Thing As A Free Lunch (TANSTAAFL). You are the greatest single influence in your universe, and your life is the result of *your* actions.

"**Awareness and Consciousness**" are separate phenomena, and the consciousness of a human being is the highest form of consciousness that we know. Despite our universally intimate experience with consciousness, nobody has ever been able to quantify its exact nature.

You learned about "**Crafting Spells**" and "**Casting Spells**" in order to change your world. It starts with being able to visualize the desired result and believing the result can come to pass. You then learned to write the result down and include specific information.

"**Psychology**" is all very good, but it has its limitations. It provides sufficient explanation for *some* people, but might not be enough for most people.

"**Physics,**" by definition, must be able to explain everything in the universe, including consciousness and otherwise "magical" results. It explains the sufficiently advanced technology that makes magic work. Your mobile phone is an example. Most importantly, you should realize your body is composed of matter that exists in many dimensions. It's not just your consciousness that you cannot see; you are unable to completely see *anything* made of matter in the entire universe, including your own body. Finally, what you perceive as "change over time" might actually be "perception of change as we move through multiple 3-branes (universes).

Doing the Impossible

Let's go back to our little exercise – the one where you lifted your hand. We already discussed some of the mechanics of that process, from the neural activity in your brain and nervous system down to the chemical activity of the neurotransmitters, which in turn leads to a phenomenal array of submicroscopic events that number in the trillions. This all happens in a split second.

This is not something you can do. Seriously—I have a great deal of respect for the human brain and consciousness itself, but it just doesn't have that kind of ability. There are simply too many things happening.

The classical explanation is that you are not manipulating submicroscopic events any more than you are turning the crankshaft in your car engine; you just press on one pedal and the car speeds up, press the other pedal and the car slows down. You don't need to know how the engine works. Let's examine this process.

This explanation implies that we initiate a certain number of actions, after which a critical mass is reached and the remaining events occur automatically, thus leading to an inevitable conclusion—hopefully, a close approximation to the desired result. In the case of the car, we apply a certain amount of pressure to the accelerator pedal. In a fuel-injected, internal-combustion powered vehicle, this opens a butterfly valve in the throttle body that allows air to enter the intake manifold, thus decreasing the manifold vacuum. Various sensors detect the airflow through the throttle body as well as the manifold vacuum level and report those data to the computer, which then directs the fuel injectors to inject a specific amount of fuel to specific cylinders at specific times. The specifics are calculated from the sensors on the air intake side we just mentioned (which predict the future of the combustion chamber); sensors on the exhaust side (which report the immediate results of past combustions in the chamber)[1]; and also sensors that report the position of the moving parts of the engine and the speed of those moving parts. When the fuel and air are in the cylinder, and everything is in the proper position, the computer directs electric current (tens of thousands of volts) to the spark plug, which ignites the fuel/air mixture, which results in the explosion that provides the power to accelerate the car.

The problem with using a technical analogy to consciousness is that the car (or other technology) did not assemble itself, and we didn't just find it in a field and learn to drive it by trial and error. It took the collective efforts of mankind thousands of years to master the necessary array of technologies to create the modern

---

[1] Notice that by viewing the immediate past and predicting the immediate future, these sensors provide the engine control module a virtual four-dimensional view of the engine operation.

automobile. We observed nature and developed technologies to exploit natural behavior. Every step of the way, some human consciousness either envisioned a new application for an existing technology, or by observing existing technology, envisioned a *new* technology that improved on what came before. Henry Ford had to build the Model T before Enzo Ferrari could build his Redhead—er, Testa Rossa. Technology is ultimately the *result* of consciousness, and using technology as an analogy to explain consciousness is a circular reference. In the case of the car, each event leading to the acceleration of the car can be explained in great detail as the inevitable result of natural physical reactions to specific stimuli, except one: consciousness.

Recall the earlier discussion with regard to your brain activity and the question of whether the brain activity came first, or the thought? We know when a neuron "fires," it activates the adjacent neuron, and we can also explain and predict most of the neurological and muscular activity that ultimately results in raising your hand in the air. This is because we have observed and measured this activity. By inserting probes in your nerves and muscles and applying electric current, we can cause certain muscles to twitch in ways that cause your hand to rise into the air. Thus, in the case of raising your hand, each of the events leading to the hand lifting into the air can be explained in great detail as the inevitable result of natural physical reactions to specific stimuli, except one.

The exception, in the case of the hand, is the decision (the thought that leads to *deliberate action*) that we cannot explain. The exception, in the case of the car, is the decision to press the accelerator (once again, the thought that leads to *deliberate action*) that we cannot explain. Our ability to explain cause and effect stops with the origin of the thought itself. That's the mystery.

Inside your body, the *known* processes originate as neural activity in the brain. *Most* of what happens in the brain is related to autonomous nervous function; your heart beats, your lungs breathe, and organs you never heard of do things you never imagined. *Most* of your brain activity is *not conscious*. When you think, we can measure the neural activity. What we *don't* know is what caused the activity to happen in the first place. The odds against coherent thought being a random electrochemical reaction are incalculably high.

Consciousness is what changes your eyes from a simple camera that takes in all of the light that enters the lens into a window through which you view the world. It is what *decided* to raise or not raise your hand or to press the accelerator. It is the difference between being responsive to a situation and being *deliberately* responsive to a situation. When the doctor taps your knee with a hammer and your leg kicks, that is responsive. When the soccer forward kicks the ball into the goal it is *deliberately* responsive.

♦ ♦ ♦ ♦

In the interest of fair play, I'll mention that some very smart people believe all of our actions are predetermined and there is no such thing as free will. They believe every action is the only possible response to a specific stimulus (or situation). Every single thing that ever happened was the inevitable result of the immediately preceding situation, back to the origin of the universe. There is logic in this concept; in fact, an overabundance of logic. In its simplest form, this logic simply argues there is no such thing as a random event.

There have been studies that attempt to measure the time when somebody makes a decision and compare it to the time measurable brain activity occurs, and the brain activity inevitably occurs first. The implication is that the brain activity is created by a response to stimuli, and the brain activity *causes* the thought to occur.[2]

I have several objections to arriving at this conclusion from results of these studies:

- The studies require the subject accurately report the instant a decision is made, and compare the reported time to the time of the brain activity associated with the decision (usually to raise one or the other hand, ironically enough). The first and obvious objection is the definition of "accurately." Since reporting requires brain function, there must be a lapse of time between the actual decision and the reporting of the decision, during which lapse the brain will have had plenty of time to commence firing the neurons associated with the decision.

- The process assumes the brain can multitask. In other words, the brain making the decision to raise one or the other hand must also independently observe itself making the decision in real time and be able to accurately report on its own activity.[3] The assumption is that the two processes (action and reporting

---

[2] Libet, B., Gleason, C.A., Wright, E.W., Pearl, D.K. (1983). *Time of conscious intention to act in relation to onset of cerebral activity (readiness-potential). The unconscious initiation of a freely voluntary act. Brain.* 106 (3):623–642. PMID 6640273. Also, Haggard, P. and Eimer, M. (1999). *On the relation between brain potentials and the awareness of voluntary movements. Experimental Brain Research* 126, 128–133. PMID 10333013

[3] Any woman can tell you that multitasking is not possible for any man. Any man can tell you that multitasking is not possible at all. Let's not even *start* on the subject of accurately reporting one's own activity.

the action) will not affect one another. Any scientist can tell you the act of observation affects the outcome of an experiment. In this case, the subject of the experiment is also the observer *and* reporter. This alone introduces a measurement uncertainty far exceeding the resolution precision of the test results.

- The experiments intended to measure the existence of consciousness versus stimuli rely on the existence of the independent consciousness of the subject to measure the results. This is rather self-referential, not to mention self-defeating, if you attempt to conclude from the results that there is no consciousness independent of brain activity.

- If you program the same experiment using a computer, where decision time is the moment a random number generator comes up with a certain number, after which event the computer energizes an LED and prints a time stamp. The LED will always light before the time recorded in the time stamp, simply because only one step is required to light the LED. In order to find out what time it is, the computer needs to go back into a subroutine to consult its internal clock, and then another subroutine to record the time. You would need to intentionally delay energizing the LED in order to make it light *after* the time stamp. The analogy in the brain experiment is that there are zero steps required to initiate the measured neural activity in the brain, and many steps (billions or trillions) required to externally *report* on the decision, *in addition to* repeating the same steps required to make the initial left or right decision. Thus, neural activity will *always* occur first regardless of its origin.

- The concept of neural activity preceding conscious thought does not explain why neural activity is as ordered as it is. Why do neurons fire in patterns resulting in coherent thought? Considering the virtually infinite number of possible neural sequences available in the brain, one can only mathematically conclude that a coherent thought would be highly improbable at all, much less a common occurrence.[4] Indeed, there are brains where neurons fire more or less randomly than is considered normal, resulting in abnormal actions and thoughts. We use the term *neurological disorders* when referring to these cases.

- Assume for a moment that thought *does* precede neural activity. Because the neural activity is the first physical manifestation of the thought in the mind of the observer, and the reporting activity itself *is* a physical activity, how could the observer possibly report the thought until *after* the neural activity? Once again, neural activity *must* precede reporting the activity, even though (in this case) we know it occurred last.

My final objection is more pragmatic: if everything is pre-destined, why not simply assume you have an enjoyable destiny and get on with it?

♦ ♦ ♦ ♦

Having concluded that we cannot *consciously* manage the trillions of activities required to do something as simple as raising a hand, what exactly is going on?

---

[4] Rather like locking the proverbial one hundred monkeys in a room with one hundred typewriters to see how long it takes them to generate a Shakespearian sonnet.

Living in Three Dimensions

We know we are a multidimensional being because we can see three of those dimensions and envision a fourth (time). There are profound reasons for believing there are as many as seven additional dimensions required to sustain the universe as we know it. As previously discussed, I proposed that just as we travel through multiple 1- and 2-branes (universes) by simply walking across the room, we also move through multiple *three*-dimensional universes as we move in the *ana/kata* direction along an additional vector *w*. This vector is commonly referred to as "time."

Reviewing our experiment with the ball and camera on a string, we assumed the simulated two-dimensional universes (2-branes) we were observing, as well as the three-dimensional universe (3-brane) from which we were observing, were both static (timeless). As we moved our point of view through multiple 2-branes, we saw change as the cross section of the ball expanded and then contracted. This change can be viewed as change over time from the point of view in a single 2-brane, or change over motion as the point of view moved through *multiple* 2-branes. There is no way to determine the difference; the result is exactly the same.

Using the second paradigm, instead sitting in single, three-dimensional universe (3-brane) and watching things change, we are instead moving through *multiple* 3-branes along the *w* vector (through time), and the changes we see are actually the differences between adjacent universes. This makes the assumption that each 3-brane we pass through is static (timeless).

The Flip Chart

Looking at this from a two-dimensional perspective, let's imagine a flip chart of paper. Each piece of paper represents a 2-brane (two-dimensional universe). On the bottom sheet of paper, there is a circle drawn at the bottom center, and on each overlying sheet of paper, the same circle is drawn slightly higher and to the right. On the top sheet of paper, the circle is in the upper-right corner.

If you riffle through the paper from bottom to top, you perceive the circle travels from the bottom center to the upper-right corner of the paper. The more sheets of paper we use, the smoother the motion is going to appear. The actual universe uses more sheets than you can imagine—literally. In this case, each 2-brane is timeless; nothing changes on any individual sheet. What appears to be change is when we view successive n-branes rapidly in sequential order. We interpret the differences as motion, or change.

Let's Check on the Cat

Back to Schrödinger's cat. I mentioned in passing that the experiment was meant to illustrate the challenge of quantum superposition. Quantum superposition states that a particle exists as a probability that can be mathematically calculated and predicted. The problem, as Schrödinger so eloquently observed, is that it is not a probability to the *cat*.

One answer to this dilemma is called the many worlds interpretation, or MWI. According to the MWI, at any time when the observer opens the box, predictive wave function collapses to all possibilities, and the universe splits into two continua. Thus, the observer in one continuum finds a dead cat, and the same observer in the other continuum finds a live cat.

Many Worlds Interpretation

I had a lot of trouble believing the MWI. It seemed unreasonable to me to expect the universe was peeling off doubles everywhere. It leads to some interesting concepts, such as alternate histories, but it didn't seem quite likely that there were other me's out there somewhere, somehow having made different choices. There must be several continua where I died—maybe thousands. That sucks; what would the world be like without me? And somewhere, one of me made all the right choices. What's his life like, and does he realize he left a trail of dead bodies all over the universe?

However, once I started coming to grips with the idea that there are more than three dimensions, and I realized that I can't even see most of who I think I am, this multiple universe thing started becoming a bit more palatable.

◆ ◆ ◆ ◆

An inconsistency that bothered me for quite a while was something I mentioned earlier in the book—namely, the use of the word "infinity." If there are an infinite number of points in a line, and an infinite number of lines in a plane, does that mean there are infinity-squared dimensions in the plane? That's nonsensical.

It turns out that in the case of superstring theory, the fundamental building block of the universe would be a string loop with a diameter about the size of a Planck Length. The Planck Length is about 1.616252×10^{-33} cm, give or take.[5] That's less than *.000,000,000,000,000,000,000,000,000,000,002* cm. That's freaking tiny. However, it does represent a finite number, which puts some sense back into the equations.

---

[5] Give or take a little teeny, tiny bit!

Thus, there would only be room for about 2×10^{98} 0-branes in a cube of sugar. We are still talking about incomprehensibly large (and small) numbers, but they are numbers nonetheless. However, when you start to think about the possible 1- and 2-branes that can pass *through* the sugar cube, we're pretty much off into the land of infinity again, especially if you consider that the line or the plane can bend—they do not have to be flat or straight.

I'm bringing all of this to your attention so you can realize there is a *lot* of room for extra *n*-branes (universes). *They might even exist in directions (dimensions) that you can't see[6]!* Think about it. In a single sugar cube, you might have 5×10^{360} 0-brane universes rattling around, and *each one* can exist in an even larger number of other *n*-branes. That's in a sugar cube. If you look around you, will see that an awful lot of sugar cubes will fit in known space, and that is just one of an *infinite* number of 3-brane universes.

How this applies to the MWI is that instead of new universes being created every time there is more than one possible state, there is one universe where *all of the possible states already exist.* What we observe is simply a result of where we *travel* in that universe.

---

[6] All of the dimensions exist at each point (zero-dimensional universe) possibly rolled up into what is called a Calabi-Yau manifold. It follows that the string would follow the folds of the Calabi-Yau manifold that occupies any given zero-dimensional location. When the string vibrates, it represents energy (and/or mass). Like a string in our three-dimensional universe, each of the manifold strings can vibrate in none, one, or more dimensions (represented by a dimensional fold).

The Multiverse

One of the difficulties that physicists and astronomers have had in explaining the universe is that there are certain constants (like "*C*") that just have no rational explanation; they just seem to *be*. Where this becomes a problem is that if you change these constants, it completely changes, well, the whole universe. Stuff like gravity won't work and matter cannot exist. So, the scientists have been essentially saying, "Gee, I'm really happy that this all works and everything, but *why?*"[7]

Recently, scientists have begun to realize and accept as mainstream thought that as we look in the sky and through our most powerful telescopes, the magnificent cosmos that we see is not *the* universe, but just one of an infinite number of universes that is now being referred to as the Multiverse. Given there are an infinite number of universes, everything is certain to exist, and we happen to be living in the universe with these particular rules.

In this book, we have been using the language of *n*-branes that are a part of a single, multi-dimensional universe (where "*n*" represents the number of dimensions) instead of saying "Multiverse," but they are essentially the same concept.

Pages

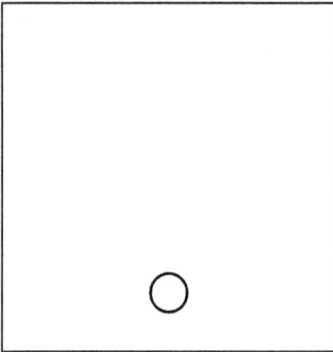

Figure 15- 1. *The Flip Chart*

Start with the first page of our flip chart (Figure 15-1). This

---

[7] They are beginning to think like engineers!

single sheet represents a static two-dimensional universe (2-brane) unaffected by time. Nothing changes. As we move to the next sheet in the stack, we don't know what is going to happen. Quantum mechanics states there is a possibility that *anything* might happen!

The first sheet has a circle at the bottom center. The circle is composed of black points, and white points make up the blank space. In the real universe, each point in space is occupied by a string that either is vibrating or not, and the characteristics of the vibration determine what the string represents (e.g., electron, neutrino, or quark). For the sake of simplicity, let's assume our points can only be either black or white.

As we imagine the composition of the next sheet in our flip chart, there are only two options for each point on the sheet—resulting in a 50 percent chance of any given point being black. The sheet would be some shade of grey—about half the points would be black and the rest would be white. That would be equivalent to the universe blowing up; nothing would be left but static. Fortunately, that is not the case. Quantum mechanics predicts *probabilities,* but they are not random probabilities. There are rules that govern the probability for the state of any adjacent particle (vibrating string).

When you pluck a guitar string, the adjacent strings also vibrate, and the same is true for our particle strings. Energy *moves.* There are small probabilities that something unusual might occur (resulting in what seems like a random event), but for the most part, the probabilities are very significant for the state of any point in the adjacent universe (the next sheet of our flip chart).

Let's throw a bit of probability into our imaginary universe (the flip chart), and specify that in sequential pages (2-branes), at any given black point on the first page, the corresponding point on the second page is 90 percent likely to be black. For a white point *adjacent to* a black point on the first page, the corresponding point on the second page is 99 percent likely to be black (the circle is going to want to *move*). For a white point adjacent only to other white points on the first page (zero energy), there is only a .001 percent likelihood of being black.

There are also rules for the circle itself—it *likes* being a circle, and has a very high probability of holding its shape and form to very close tolerances. If the shape is composed of one million points (particles) in a circle, on the second sheet there will be one million points in the shape of a circle, with a very small probability of deviation. These rules are true for all subsequent pages as we go up the stack.

Two things are likely to happen: (1) because there is a higher probability for adjacent white points to become black, the circle is likely to move relative to its position on the first page; and (2) it is very unlikely (not impossible) that other circles will randomly appear.

This sounds a bit complicated, and in the real universe, things are indeed quite complex. The idea here is to realize that there are *rules* determining the likely state of given points in adjacent *universes*. These rules are expressed as probabilities.

Behavior

What happens when we apply these rules to our pieces of paper? As we flip from one page to the next, the circle will probably move in some direction or it may not move at all. We won't know until we look – very much like the cat in the box. If quantum mechanics applied to our piece of paper, the points on the second sheet of

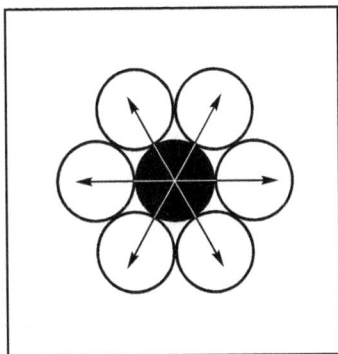

Figure 15- 2. *Possible directions*

paper (the adjacent 2-brane) would be in a state of quantum superposition until somebody bothered to look.

Here's where the many worlds interpretation comes in to play. According to the MWI, the circle moves in *every possible direction* in multiple succeeding universes. If we look at an individual black point, and pack the possible directions it may move as tightly as possible (see Figure 15-2), it appears there would be six possible directions for the point to move in adjacent universes. That means there are seven possible adjacent universes, counting the possibility that the circle doesn't move at all.

"This is a stack of paper" you say. "*What* seven different adjacent universes? There can only be two; one on top and one on bottom. In fact, if we are going in one direction (bottom to top), there would only be *one* adjacent universe in that direction, right?"

The answer is "no." Remember each page may be only two dimensions, but all of the pages combined actually exist in three dimensions, and from the point of view on any single page, there is no way to see any other page.

According to the MWI, there are seven circles on seven different sheets of paper out there somewhere, each one representing the seven different possible positions (see Figure 15-3). I've exaggerated and labeled the motion for clarity.

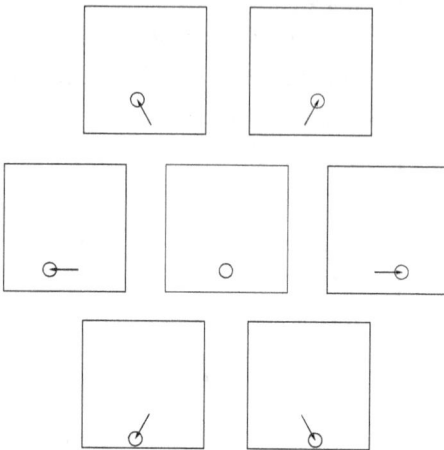

Figure 15- 3. *Possible alternatives*

Before we flip the page, there are seven possible options for the following page. We select *one* of those pages. It doesn't matter which one because they are all equally probable. That choice nails down the particular continuum for us as an observer (if this involved two-dimensional cats, there would almost certainly be a fatality, which is why we are not using cats in this particular exercise). We then move on to the next seven possibilities that become available as a result of our first selection. The others are still there, but we aren't going to use them in our flip chart. They will go into somebody else's flip chart.

Here's where it gets interesting. If we program our rules into a computer and let it randomly select one of the seven possibilities for each successive page, we would see the circle move all over the place. It might stay in place and vibrate, or move slowly or quickly, and occasionally not move at all. There is a very remote chance that a new circle may pop up (remember the .001 percent probability?), and there is also a remote possibility the circle could vanish. Eventually, the circle would manage to wander to every possible location in the confines of the page.

That is hardly a satisfying result, so let's throw something in the mix to make it more interesting. Let's show the computer a sheet with the circle drawn at the upper-right corner and direct the computer to achieve that result. We do so by programming a bias—an additional probability—to select the subsequent sheet where the circle is closest to the example sheet.

What will then happen is, *no matter how small the bias*, the computer will draw a cartoon showing motion similar to Figure 15-4. There will likely be small detours – remember, *anything* is still possible. These will most likely be limited to a bit of wiggle in the course. Stronger bias (probability) will result in fewer deviations and a straighter line.

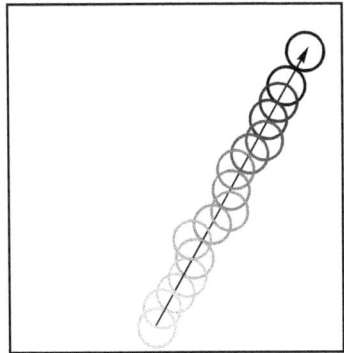

Figure 15- 4. *Introducing bias.*

Rationale

Why would we program a bias into the computer? Well, mainly because watching a cartoon circle bounce around a paper square gets pretty boring after a while. If you are the observer and your goal is to end up with the circle in the upper-right corner, which paper from the choices in Figure 15-3 would you put on the stack? We all like to solve puzzles, and this is a pretty simple one; you'd pick the best answer with few deviations.

Application

Putting this into perspective, if each page of our flip chart represents a 2-brane, by observing (either you or the computer program are the observer) a desired result you can easily *achieve* the desired result by selecting the best intermediate 2-branes between the current (present) and final (future) 2-branes.

Here's the important bit: *this is only possible when viewing from a higher-order dimension.* In other words, you can make an intelligent choice about which of the seven possible pages to select only if you can view all seven alternatives from a three-dimensional point of view. You pick one most closely corresponding to your desired result. When you move on to that page, the next set of choices become available, and you make the next selection.

If the circle represents your right hand, your consciousness, observing from higher order dimensions, is selecting the next 3-brane based on which option is closest to the desired destination, namely your right hand being up in the air. It doesn't have to actually make stuff happen—*every possible thing happens.* Your consciousness just has to select the immediate future closest to your desired result. You visualize your right hand in the air, and the next 3-brane (three dimensional universe) your consciousness chooses is the one closest to the universe with your right hand in the air, and it keeps on choosing them until the hand is in the air.

That's *way* easier than trying to coordinate trillions of separate events.

Boxes

Imagine a true three-dimensional universe—one without time.[8] Everything would stand absolutely still, and absolutely nothing would change. This is the three-dimensional analogy to the page in our previous exercise, except we would be visualizing a box instead of a sheet of paper, and our universe is a lot more complicated than a black circle on a white piece of paper. However, the complexity is irrelevant, because at any particular point the superstring particle will have a finite set of possible states. There are lots more of them, but they all obey the same rules and are subject to the same probabilities.

Using the application mentioned a moment ago, you and I are watching the three dimensions we can either directly sense or imagine, and flying through adjacent universes at nearly our C quota, similar to flipping through the pages on our flip chart. We have established that it is likely that our *consciousness* functions in the higher-order dimensions. Even though we can *sense* in only one dimension at a time, our brain aggregates all of the information it receives into a multidimensional picture we perceive with our conscious mind.

♦ ♦ ♦ ♦

Here's the thing: I believe it is naïve to assume that information carried by photons is present only in the three dimensions we use to visualize our world. The assumptions are that there are many dimensions (directions) and any particular point is going to exist in all of those dimensions. There is no particular prohibition that says a photon can travel in *only three of*

---

[8] Okay. I *know* that if time really stood still, I wouldn't be able to see anything. This part is make-believe. Let's pretend that we still have light.

the many available directions. It can travel in any direction, depending on the trigger that set it on its way (the action part of Newton's statement, *"Every action has an equal and opposite reaction"[9]*).

As living creatures, there are things we need to do to survive. We have already discussed the different levels of awareness and consciousness. We know our consciousness is superior to the consciousness of animals, and that different animals have different levels of consciousness (not to be confused with intelligence, which is entirely different).

We sense what we need to sense in order to survive. Bees see far into the ultraviolet; we don't because we don't need to. Cats can see very well in the dark; we don't because we don't need to. Most people can see more colors than dogs. Color is important to us, but not to dogs. On the other hand, dogs can smell a lot more things than us. The interesting thing is that all of the critters mentioned *get the same information.* The same light reaches our eyes; we breathe in the same smells. It all comes down to the simple concept that we have adapted to sense those things that are necessary to our survival as a species, but not a whole lot more, despite the fact that it would be very cool to be able to see and smell all of that very interesting stuff!

So far, humans have been able to survive by physically observing a three-dimensional world. That doesn't mean that we don't get information from other dimensions, any more than it means ultraviolet light doesn't reach our eyes. Ultraviolet light

---

[9] The third of the three laws of motion set forth in Isaac Newton's *Philosophiae Naturalis Principia Mathematica,* "When one body exerts a force on a second body, the second body simultaneously exerts a force equal in magnitude and opposite in direction on the first body."

does reach our eyes; we just have no use for it, so it doesn't register. Bees, on the other hand, require the ability to see in ultraviolet light in order to spot their favorite flower.

However, there is no reason to assume that we *mentally* function in only three dimensions. In fact, one of the things that really separates us from animals is our ability to mentally and *consciously* "see" into the fourth dimension: time.

Mankind, as opposed to most animals, spends the vast majority of its life operating in a dimension it cannot perceive. As far as I know, humans are the only animals that have jobs. For that matter, we are the only animals that *offer* jobs. Why do we have jobs? So we can buy food, shelter, transportation, to attract a suitable mate, and so forth.

Taking into account that a lot of people don't even *like* their jobs, why do we do that? The reason is because we can easily picture an unpleasant future if we had no income. For most of us, having a job equals having an income. The reason we take new jobs or new responsibilities is because we can picture a more pleasant future if we do those things. That makes sense, but it begs the question, "If it's such a great idea, why don't other animals plan for the future?"

The better question is, "How do we know the future even *exists?*"

The kneejerk answer is that it is intuitively obvious, but that explanation is no more valid for us any more than it is for Bomb #20. I propose an alternative answer.

We know that photons (information) can travel in any direction from any source. We also know that we receive vast amounts of information that do not register with our senses. Is it possible that we are also receiving information (photons) traveling from adjacent universes (3-branes)? In particular, the ones from the general direction that we are traveling?

I look out the window and I see the house across the street. The house itself is not generating photons (well, not many, and I can't really see the ones it does generate).[10] What I'm seeing are the photons that originated on the sun that smacked right into the side of that building. It absorbed a lot of them, but the brick-colored ones with yellow trim bounced right off and flew into my eyeballs. Somebody else down the street can *also* see that same house, which means there are gazillions of brick-colored photons with yellow trim flying every which way.

And by every which way, I mean *every* which way. Just like you and me, the matter that makes up that house across the street exists in just as many dimensions as you and me. Some of those photons are going up, down, and across the street, and time being just another dimension, there's no reason some of them can't be headed up and down the *w* dimension in both the *ana* (future) and *kata* (past) directions.

In fact, the photons I'm seeing actually left that house a fraction of a second ago, right? Wouldn't that mean that the photons I'm seeing actually would need to travel in a vector that not only crossed the street but also up the time stream in the *ana* direction a little ways?

Time for another beer; you need to think about that for a minute. Imagine trying to shoot one of the moving targets in a

---

[10] If you've ever had a Geiger counter and wandered around with it, you know that bricks are radioactive. Not very much, mind you, but hey, a photon is a photon. You could use a brick for your diabolical mechanism, I suppose, but based on the readings I saw, your cat wouldn't last even a couple of seconds, if that long. You could very well end up gassing *yourself* before you got the lid on.

carnival shooting gallery with a BB gun. If you aim at the target and pull the trigger, you will miss, because the target moved out of the way while the BB was traveling from the gun. In order to hit the target, you need to aim *ahead* of the target, so the BB and the target arrive at the same place at the same time.

If the photons from the house just vectored directly across the street and I'm traveling at nearly the speed of light myself across multiple universes, I wouldn't even *be* in that universe when the photon got to my house. There wouldn't even be a house, because, thankfully, it came along with me instead of waiting around for some stupid photon.

Remember back in chapter 10 we established that *all* of your sensory input is from the past, whether it be tiny fractions of a second to billions of years in the case of looking at a distant galaxy. Think of the photon like the BB and your eye as the moving target. In order to hit the target, you don't aim at the target; you aim at *where the target is going to be* when the BB gets there.[11] The photons that reach your eyeballs do so because they traveled the correct vector across the *x, y, z, and w* dimensions.

So, it's pretty obvious that a bunch of photons flew *up* the time stream. We observe photons that originated in our past; in fact, they are the only ones we *can* see. However, there's no reason to believe they couldn't fly *down* the time stream as well, which means that we are surrounded by photons from the future. We just aren't looking in the right direction. There's a good reason for that.

◆ ◆ ◆ ◆

Going back to our flip chart, think of it as a spacetime continuum. If you riffle through the pages, the circle moves,

---

[11] Please don't be aiming BB guns at anybody's eyes!

depending on where it is located on successive pages. However, in order to do that, the circles already need to exist.

On any page that represents any particular instant, all of the possibilities (one out of seven possibilities in our simple example) have collapsed into a specific state. The circle is in one place and one place only. Think about the past and the future in terms of our flip chart. In terms of the spacetime, the past is already drawn, and we could in theory replay the entire continuum by riffling through the pages.

The future is a different matter. There isn't a next page; there are 7 next pages. There isn't a page-after-next; there are 49 pages after the next 7, and 2,401 pages after those 49. In just those couple of pages, there is too much information for us to process, even in just a little two-dimensional flip chart. The universe is more than two dimensions, and there are more than seven possible directions, even taking inertia into account (the fact that we have momentum in a particular direction is going to eliminate the vast majority of possibilities). In our case, the number of possible energy-neutral options[12] will probably be equal to the number of existing dimensions (i.e., "many" in troll-speak).

The corollary to the principle of *focus* (as described in chapter 9) is to *filter*. At some point, the light reflected from all of the blue things in the room entered your eyes. The reason you don't remember most of them is because your brain decided it simply didn't need that information. If you stored everything that comes

---

[12] In our two-dimensional flip chart, if we have momentum and are traveling from the bottom of the chart toward the goal (north, northeasterly), the options would be the two at the top-right of Figure 15-4. All of the other options would require making a sharp turn, coming to a complete stop, or reversing direction, all of which would require additional energy.

into your eyes, your brain would be so cluttered with useless information that you would be unable to access the important stuff when you needed it. Thus, your brain filters out what appears to be useless information at the time and only remembers the subject of your focus. Have you ever been driving down a highway and realized you don't actually know where you are, or that you can't remember anything at all about the last ten miles? Your conscious mind is fully focused on processing the masses of information needed to drive safely, but none of it has anything to do with the rest of your life, so it is completely filtered out.

If your brain were to try to process all of the information you are receiving from all of the possible alternative futures, you would be instantly overwhelmed, so most of that information is discarded. I do think that humans and most other conscious animals actually *do* process information from that vector, but only from a short distance upstream. Have you ever been able to see the results of an event before it happened? Sometimes, we're just like a "deer in the headlights," and other times we react so quickly to avoid a disaster we can't believe our own good fortune. I think the difference might be that in that split-second, we either could or could not see a clear path at hand.

The only thing we *can* do is pick the most suitable of the available options that represent the next instant in our space–time continuum. With no specific destination in mind, it would be like our computer program with no bias. Events would tend to be random, and we'd bounce from one situation to another with no apparent reason.

You might think this is not a terribly bad description of your life, but that's not quite true. Truly random directions would result in *no* continuity in your life at all. Remember the loaf of bread?

You need the grocer, the truck driver, the baker, and the farmer to exist in your universe in order for you to have your bread.

They need you, too. Remember, we are *all* creating our futures. You are aiming for a world with bread-on-demand, and they are aiming for a world where people buy bread, so everybody together is creating the collective continuum you are experiencing. That's the wild magic—that's what nobody has told you about (until now). This collective visualization is why we have continuity, while at the same time experiencing so much chaos. The collective vision of billions of people has led to the continuum we currently experience. Among those billions are those who have a clear vision of *their* future and pull the rest of us along with them.

Bundles

Like our computer program that follows rules to determine the placement of the circle in adjacent pages, there are similar rules governing the behavior of mass in adjacent universes—*any* adjacent universes—particularly with regard to motion. As mass and/or velocity in a particular direction increases for a particular point in n-dimensional space, there are increasingly spectacular probabilities for adjacent points in other dimensions.

Think of dropping a bowling ball from about twelve inches directly over your toes. You can predict a lot of things—like where the bowling ball is going to land, what it will do to your toes—and can even go so far as predicting which of the stronger epithets you will use. Rules are *rules.* Quantum superposition my

Aunt Fanny; that thing is going to *hurt* when it lands, I don't care how many subatomic particles ended up somewhere else.[13]

Adjacent 3-branes are very similar with very small differences; exactly like the circle in our flip chart that is in a slightly different location as we move from page to page.

◆ ◆ ◆ ◆

I'd like to pause at this point to discuss time once again. Time travel is one of mankind's persistent fantasies. If, as I'm suggesting, we are moving through different universes and these universes exist in a timeless state, shouldn't we be able to go back in time, rather like thumbing through our flip chart backward?

Well, the answer is yes and no. This is indeed possible, and like our flip chart, we should be able to go back as well as forward. It's a question that has bothered a lot of very smart people. Here are some things to think about.

Number 1: We are moving at nearly the speed of light, in the *ana* direction along the *w* axis. Remember the whole inertia business? Once you let go of the bowling ball, in order to go back in time to just *before* you dropped the ball, you have to come to a dead stop from nearly the speed of light, completely reverse course, and then accelerate back along the *w* axis in the *kata* direction to get back to the point just before you let go of the ball. That's pretty much breaking every rule that we know about mass, energy, and bowling balls. It would be far easier to reverse the course of a speeding train by throwing a feather at the front of it. Actually, at the velocities we are traveling, throwing a feather would be *considerably* more likely to stop a train dead in its tracks.

---

[13] Quantum superposition suggests there is a remote possibility that the bowling ball will land in the middle of Antarctica. Don't count on it.

Besides, even if you managed to turn back time and got back to the starting point, and then went through all of the business of turning back in the right direction again, you are *still* in the same universe you were before, and you're just going to do the same thing anyway.

Number 2: Having eliminated the possibility of instantaneous reversal of direction, consider the possibility of just changing direction a little bit so we end up in a universe where the bowling ball completely misses your foot. *That's* easy enough to do by just yanking your foot out of the way. On the cosmic scale of things, this is something you can easily accomplish in the time it takes for the bowling ball to reach your toes.

If you are really still hung up on time travel and very ambitious, you might think, "Why can't I loop back around and come back at that universe again?"

Well, that is entirely possible, except for that pesky inertia business again. Moving your foot out from under the bowling ball doesn't take a whole lot of energy, mainly because the foot is *also* traveling pretty much at the same speed and direction as the rest of you. Accelerating a kilo of mass a couple of inches is no big deal. On the other hand, to move your entire self in a complete circle in the *ana* and *kata* directions through uncharted dimensions actually *is* a pretty big deal. You are talking about causing the full deflection of significant mass moving nearly the speed of light, a task requiring an enormous expenditure of energy.

If you were an aircraft carrier traveling at maximum velocity at sea, you could crank the rudder and the ship would begin to turn, but only slowly. Once you established the maximum rate of turn for your speed, you could hold it and then begin to straighten out as you got to the starting point. The turn is *not* going to happen on a dime; it is going to use a lot of ocean, and although you might end up very close to your initial location and direction, it's almost certain to be slightly off.

In your case, the bowling ball already fell on your toes and you will most likely die of old age long before you got back to the start. Besides, you could never really return to the *exact same* continuum, because the older, wiser you isn't *in* that continuum. If you were, you wouldn't need to return to it, you would already be there. So, you'd be in a different continuum, and all you could do is stupidly watch yourself drop a bowling ball on your foot. Perhaps you could prevent that, but then the both of yous[14] would be wandering off in a completely different spacetime continuum.

Number 3: What about traveling *forward* in time? Well, yes, we *are* doing that, aren't we? In fact, we are pretty much at the speed limit. Even if we could skip ahead somehow, we'd have the same problems as before with regard to coming back. Good luck on that one.

Number 4: What about wormholes and all those really cool things that might allow us to travel to another universe? The appeal of those phenomena has to do with instantaneous travel to a spatially distant location in spacetime. This would enable us to study distant things as they are, not as they were. It might also allow for real-time communication to distant stars, or possibly even real-time interstellar travel.

However, I don't think those types of spatial curiosities, exciting as they are, are going to allow us to travel back in time to once and for all confirm the facts of the assassination of JFK or get a video recording of the Battle of Thermopylae. Besides, it's

---

[14] Maybe we could call this new continuum "New Jersey."

already been established that the act of observation has an impact on what is being observed. No matter where or when you went, it would be a different continuum than one where you were not present.

◆ ◆ ◆ ◆

Returning to *our* universes (3-branes), we were discussing the concept that the differences between adjacent 3-branes are very small. As we travel through the dimensions, we see a coherent change of state from one 3-brane to the next, because there is so little change from one 3-brane to an adjacent 3-brane.

That's not to say there aren't surprises. Perhaps you lose your job—that might be a big surprise, but it's not as though your company simply vanished. It's still there, and everything seems to be humming right along despite your personal circumstances. In terms of cosmic significance, however, your job doesn't amount to much, no matter how indispensable you think you are.

For a two-dimensional perspective, we can visualize multiple 2-brane universes as a flip chart where we can see the change by riffling through the pages.

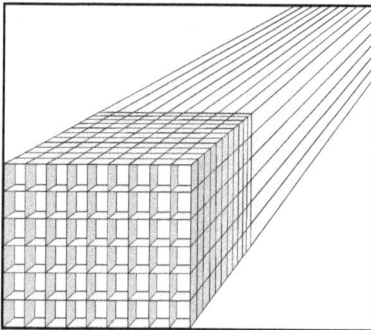

Figure 15- 5. *Stacked 3-branes*

For a three-dimensional perspective, visualize the 3-brane universes as boxes stacked on one another, side-to-side and front-to-back (Figure 15-5). Instead of riffling through pages, visualize a path that follows from one box to an adjacent box.

The line (or continuum) described by this path would look like a chord (Figure 15-6). If we imagine many different continua, it would be represented by bundle of chords similar to a rope (Figure 15-7).

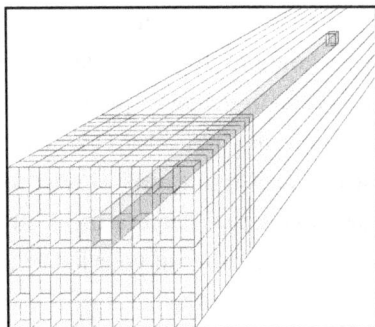

Figure 15- 6. *A continuum*

When we imagine alternate universes, we are thinking of a bundle like this. The cords closest to each other in the bundle are the most similar continua. Note that a continuum can change direction, overlap, or even pass through other continua. This depends on which of several available boxes the continuum takes as it moves forward, taking into account physical factors such as inertia.

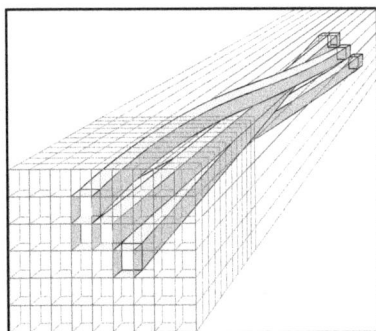

Figure 15- 7. *A bundle*

Back to Our Exercise

Returning to our exercise, you chose to raise one hand or the other, neither, or both—four possibilities. A moment ago, I explained how our consciousness operating from a three dimensional perspective could select the best among seven possible intermediate 2-branes by choosing the alternative closest to the desired result (a circle in the upper-right corner).

In the case of our exercise, I had you *first* decide what you were going to do—the desired result. Your consciousness (which resides in dimensions beyond the three we can observe) used that decision as the observed desired result and selected which particular 3-brane was closest to the desired result and kept on selecting until it reached the desired result, and one or both of your hands were either in your lap or in the air.

The whole business of the trillions of events leading to the result was *not* initiated by your conscious (or subconscious) mind.

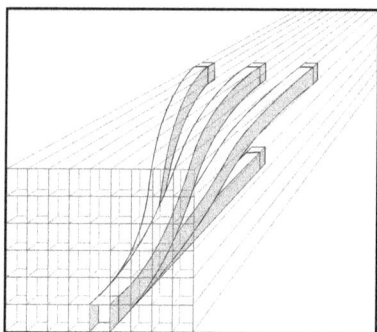

Figure 15- 8. *Four options*

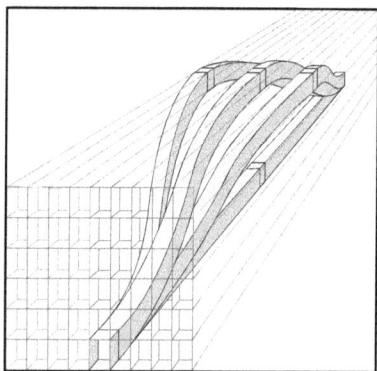

Figure 15-9. *Convergence*

There was simply a 3-brane universe closer to the desired result, and your conscious mind chose to observe that particular 3-brane. That 3-brane happened to be one where those trillions of events were initiated. Like moving your foot out from under the bowling ball, raising your hand is not a monumental undertaking. The deflection of the continuum you are following consumed no energy at all; in your direction of travel, there were several choices, each as close as the next—you simply picked a course that took you where you wanted to go (Figure 15-8).

Because the course correction was so tiny (on the cosmic scale of things), it's likely the four possible continuums in this case could merge back into one because it simply didn't matter what you did (Figure 15-9).

What is interesting about this concept is it illustrates that your consciousness, observing from a higher-order dimension, may be able to select among multiple choices as you were able to do with the flip chart. It can also select subsequent choices so the end result is the same destination; there's more than one way to get from point A to point B. This allows you to correct course if your continuum deviates from an optimum path for any reason, including the effects caused by the choices of other people in your universe.

Back to Our Meeting

Let's go back to the meeting with one hundred people. I'm the speaker, and in this particular continuum, I zipped my fly, thank you very much.

When the one hundred of us are in the closed auditorium, we are in the same continuum. In our bundle, there are several, possibly many nearly identical meetings in continua adjacent to ours. They are all a little bit different; maybe I didn't check my trousers in a few of them; maybe the Norwegian and Japanese fellows recognized each other, stopped off for a drink, and didn't show up—who knows? For now, though, the doors are shut, and we are all sharing the trip through the universe for a little while.

Suddenly, toward the middle of the presentation and without warning, I say, "Let's do a little exercise!"

I just set off a cluster bomb of new continua. In one continuum, nobody raised their hands at all, and I felt really stupid. In another, everybody raised both hands and I felt like it was a gospel revival. In two continua, you were the only person who raised a hand and you felt pretty sheepish, but in *one* continuum, everybody sat there while you raised *both* hands and you were so embarrassed it left emotional scars, and you never volunteered to raise your hands again (sorry about that).

In fact, the simple little exercise among one hundred people taking one of four possible choices results in possible continua too numerous to count! It would be something on the order of $1.6069380442589902755419620923412 \times 10^{60}$, whatever *that* means. As it probably did with the four continua when it was just you reading the book, this huge number will probably merge back down to a reasonably sized bundle. After all, it's not going to make a whole lot of difference on the cosmic scale of things.

The interesting thing about this thought experiment is that while you had complete control over *your* universe, when it came down to push and shove, which particular one of the huge number of continua you ended up observing came down to a matter of chance. In other words—you can make your choice, and that narrows the playing field a *lot*—something on the order of $1.2052035331942427066564715692559 \times 10^{60}$ fewer continua with which to contend—but you were then pretty much at the mercy of what the other people in the room wanted to do, coupled with probability. When the exercise was over, the waveforms collapsed, and the quantum superposition was resolved. *From there*, you once again have some directional control.

Getting What You Want Out of Life

If you visualize your life—the continuum you are observing—in terms of the bundle of continua, you can picture your ability to influence the direction you take through the labyrinth of continua. Based on our previous discussion, you will also see that others around you also have a bearing on your continuum. At any given point, though, you always have the option to select one particular direction over another—sort of *leaning* in the direction you choose. Over time (or distance, as the case may be), this influence has a dramatic effect on your course. Your current direction, inertia, and external influences are going to limit the *rate* of change you can experience, but you can definitely effect a change.

For this reason, you are not likely to wake up in a mansion with servants all around you tomorrow morning unless you already woke up like that this morning. Perhaps there is a continuum with you living in a mansion nearby, but it would take a really hard left turn to get there, so it's just not going to happen overnight—it would require too much energy for such a radical change in direction.

On the other hand, there might be a location far enough ahead that if your consciousness consistently *selects* in the appropriate direction, the succession of 3-branes where you live in a mansion will become part of your continuum. In terms of the direction you are currently traveling, it's not straight ahead. However, if you can visualize what you want, your consciousness will be able to "see" the direction you need to go and start steering you into successive 3-branes that bring you closer to the destination image. The change will be small at first but will gradually build up, as in the diverging continua of Figure 15-8. As you depart from your original vector, things will become increasingly different. The trip you take may involve some really strange and unexpected events.

Until Now

You are traveling through time and space, and the most powerful influence on the direction you're traveling is your own consciousness. So far, however, you've probably been just "going with the flow," so to speak, which means you have been affected by the consciousness of others to a large degree. What you expected and visualized was probably much the same as what everybody around you expected and visualized *for* you. After all, nobody ever actually mentioned that you have the ability to choose what happens in your universe, did they? Any direction you gave was probably completely accidental, or possibly coincidental. The probability is very high that some of the direction you gave was not very good at all. And if you *did* have some idea that you could craft your world, you probably didn't have any idea how it worked.

As we noted from our meeting, even when you make your choice and choose your direction, the choices of others are going to have an effect on which continuum you follow. When you were first born, you were born into the continuum that was determined by your parents. As you grew, there were more and more influences determining the road you traveled – friends, school, television—and the choices you made involving those. As you became an adult, there was probably a fairly abrupt time when your parents were no longer the single major factor in determining your direction. If you decided to go to college, well, off you went. If they decided to move to a retirement community in Arizona, then off they went.

Still, for most of us, the decisions we made were small, and the vast majority of the directional input we gave to our lives was very short term. Even those long-term goals (we often refer to them as dreams) seem to fade as we give more directional control over to surrounding circumstances. We've put our ship on autopilot and gone asleep at the wheel.

From Now On

Earlier, I used the analogy of a boat afloat in the sea. To use the same analogy, as babies, we are basically tied to our parents' boats and otherwise adrift at the mercy of the wind and current. At some point, we pick up the paddle. This would be something at the level of animal consciousness. With a paddle, you can point the boat in a particular direction and even make some progress[15], but for the most part, the wind and current are going to determine where the boat ends up.

With our ability to envision a future, our human consciousness gives us a sail and removable keel in addition to the paddle. Unfortunately, the boat didn't come with instructions, and most of us simply haven't any idea what to do with the tools we have. What knowledge we have we pass along to those who follow and have thus been advancing the human condition through the ages. Collectively, humans have made phenomenal progress as a race and continue to do so at an ever-accelerating pace. We are all beneficiaries of that collective progress. In the end, though, we're all working the paddle really hard, but the wind and current really have the biggest say in where we are going as individuals.

In the chapters on Crafting and Casting "Spells," I've given you definite steps you can use to steer your boat—to drop the keel and raise the sail, and literally navigate your path through the

---

[15] For instance, if you are a cat, you can paddle over to that loaf of bread. For the record, I was momentarily distracted and the cat tortured another loaf of bread before I could complete this manuscript. He's very fast.

multitude of universes to end up in the continuum you desire. Here are the steps, once again, for review.

1. Create the complete picture of what you want.
2. Figure out the date this should happen.
3. Write it down.

Let's look at these in light of what we have discussed since then.

1. Create the complete picture of what you want.

a. **Be very specific about what you want to happen:** By now, you should realize what you are doing. Out of virtually infinite possibilities, you are guiding yourself to a particular one. The more specific you are, the more likely you are going to get where you want to be. Be as detailed and specific about the characteristics and surroundings as possible.

b. **Be very specific about what you are giving in return (TANSTAAFL):** If you are expecting everything to stay the same while you go careening off through unknown universes, you are seriously mistaken. *Everything* is going to change! Even things that seemingly have nothing to do with your goal might happen. This includes, but is not limited to, what things you are going to do, give up, or change about your own life. It's best that *you* choose what you plan to give up. Remember, there is more than one path to your destination; some of the paths might not be to your liking.

c. **Be very specific about how this affects your world after you achieve your goal:** Once you arrive, you need to figure out what you are going to do once you get there. Success is not something that happens for an instant and is gone; you are actually planning to *merge into a continuum* where you have reached your goal. You're going to want the benefits of your achievement to stick with you. Why lose a bunch of weight only to gain it back? Why find the perfect partner only to go your separate ways? Why gain financial success only to lose everything? Wouldn't you want to get rich and stay rich? Not to mention happy and healthy! In order to do that, you need to visualize the entire *continuum,* not just one particular part of it.

2. Figure out when this should happen.

By now, you should have this whole time business in perspective. A date specifies a location in a very literal sense, just as you might specify "two miles north." Your brain is filtering everything from possible futures to prevent a debilitating overload of information. You are telling your conscious mind to open the filter in order to see something specific. A network engineer might say he is opening a pinhole in the firewall, so to speak. If you don't specify a date, you are essentially saying, "Take the exit off Interstate 10 and turn left."

A few years ago, the directions from my house to my sister's home were: go west on I-10, G-Street exit, take a left, top of the hill. If you tried to get to her house using those instructions, you'd probably give up after driving around for several hours looking for G Street. What I omitted was that G

Street was several hundred miles away and a couple of states to the west.

The date directly translates to the *distance* upstream you need to focus on in order to find the continuum where the picture you created actually exists. In order to get somewhere, you need to know what direction to go, and in order to determine the direction, you need to know where your destination is located. Once you find it, you can figure out the vector, but your consciousness needs the date in order to know where to begin looking.

3. **Write it down.**

This is a physical issue having to do with your brain. As fantastic as it is, your cerebral cortex (where you come up with all these great ideas) is pretty much squat for memory all on its own. Once you come up with the vision, you need to get it out of your head into the world where you can see it, read it, and say it. When you do this, it gets put back into your memory through sensory input and can be accessed by your consciousness. This is effectively the map your consciousness uses to choose a path to your destination.

Cooperation

Remember the hand-raising exercise among one hundred people? There were more than 1.6×10^{60} alternate possibilities in that scenario, leaving you at the mercy of ninety-nine other people. Also, remember that by choosing your own course, it reduces the possible outcomes by more than 1.2×10^{60} possibilities. That eliminates 75 percent of the possible outcomes (continua), which is an extraordinary influence, considering you are one person out of one hundred. I explained in the chapter on accountability why you are the #1 influence in your world. Even calculating the simple probabilities of your universe, it is easy to see that *you* are the most significant factor in determining your own future.

Let's examine what happens when you have another person who shares your vision. Suppose you agreed beforehand with the person seated next to you that both of you will raise two hands. What happens to the numbers then?

This reduces the possible outcomes by a total of 1.5×10^{60} possibilities. My, my, that doesn't seem to make much difference, does it? I mean, that's only 0.3×10^{60} difference from going it on your own; hardly worth mentioning, right?

Wrong. Remember there were "only" 1.6×10^{60} possibilities to begin with, and we just reduced that number by 1.5×10^{60}. In terms of percentages, acting on your own, you reduced the number of possible outcomes by 75 percent. The tiny "60" after the 10 makes it a huge number. If you had one person of like mind working with you, you could reduce the number of possible outcomes by almost 94 percent! That is serious statistical significance. In fact, with ten people working together, the possible number of outcomes is reduced by 99.9996 percent. Adding one more person (for a total of eleven), you reach the magic 99.9999 percent (six nines).[16]

The point is that while *you* are indeed the biggest factor in determining your future, you can *significantly* affect the probability of your future if somebody works with you toward the same result. When I say *significantly*, I don't mean a little bit, I mean a *lot*.

---

[16] These numbers are based on a population of one hundred with four possible choices each.

Possibly the easiest way to do this is to obtain the cooperation of your significant other. This is the best for many reasons. Here are three big ones.

- **Number 1:** what's good for the goose is good for the gander, so to speak, and vice versa. If you achieve your goal, this will impact your partner. Making the silly assumption that you share some common interests, anything that makes your life better will also make your partner's life better. If nothing else, it will provide reassurance to your partner that you are striving for a better life for *both* of you.

- **Number 2.** This is the person with whom you share your universe more than any other individual. As such, your partner is probably the #2 biggest influence in your world. Having your partner working with you on anything is a good idea. In the sea of life, your boats are tied together, so to speak. It helps *a lot* if you paddle in the same direction.

- **Number 3.** The act of clearly defining your future (and in this case, the future for both of you) will actually, for lack of better description, clearly define what the two of you actually want. This is something done by remarkably few couples. If the gander wants a mountain home, and the goose wants a beachfront cottage on the Gulf, then this is the kind of thing better known sooner than later. The solution is to craft a future with both – something both individuals will be willing to support without reservation.

The way you do this is get your partner to read the book. Don't necessarily expect your partner to be excited about it. Trust me on this; trying to explain this in-between TV shows, juggling bills, or just before bedtime is not going to work. The main reason I wrote all of this stuff down was because I just couldn't explain it any other way; there are too many concepts to digest.

Whether your partner (or you, for that matter) is skeptical is irrelevant. The idea is for each of you to craft a common vision. Then at least, the two of you have fed the same information to your consciousness. It should be an easy sell – it doesn't cost any more than a piece of paper and a little bit of quality time together.

Of course, the more people you get on board with your vision, the more powerful your vision becomes. Look at any religion, political party, or charity for that matter; it starts as one person's vision and spreads. The more people, the faster it spreads. The same collective vision can apply to a couple, a family, a sales team, or even an entire company.

Recap

- Instead of new universes being created every time there is more than one possible state, there is one universe where *all of the possible states already exist*. What we observe is a continuum, or the path we travel through the universe.

- The simple act of raising a hand involves processes at the physical, cellular, and atomic levels that number in the trillions. This is beyond the capabilities of our brains as we see it in three dimensions.

- As we travel through our spacetime continuum in a particular direction, there are several equally probable, next, future steps. If our consciousness has a particular destination in mind (such as a raised hand), it can repeatedly select the next, future step closest to the desired result until it is achieved.

- We sense time as the observation of change. In other words, we need to *think* about time, we can't simply "see" it.

- There is no particular reason that photons must travel only in the three dimensions we can infer from our senses. They can travel along any vector across any or all dimensions. Everything that we sense is the observation of photons traveling from the past.

- Unlike the single past continuum, there are so many possible future continuums we likely filter the vast majority of the information coming from that direction simply to avoid becoming overwhelmed with possibilities.

- Success Principles enable us to open a pinhole in this filter in order to locate a desired future continuum. Once we have that location, our consciousness starts selecting next, future steps that bring us closest to our desired result.

- By this process of selection, we greatly enhance our probabilities of success.

- Through the process of cooperation, we increase our probabilities by exponential factors as more and more individuals envision a common goal.

16

Conclusion

I began this all by saying, "This book tells you how to achieve what you want out of life."

The sketchy part of that statement is *"...what you want."*

Assuming you even know what you want is a pretty big assumption. It would take another entire book to help you figure that out, but even then it ends up being a very personal subject and is always (quite literally) a moving target. As I talk to people about these things, I believe their biggest obstacle to achievement is the lack of clarity and definition when they describe their future. I find that even individuals with a "clear" goal in mind often are thinking in muddy terms. Here's a list of a few:

- Graduate and get a job in *<insert field>*
- Have more money
- Pay off the bills
- Get through *<insert crisis>*
- Take a vacation this year

Hopefully by now, you will be able to see the problem with these sorts of general goals. Some of them are long-term, some are short-term, but none of them fulfill even the most basic requirements for casting a spell. Say you want a job in medicine—how about a cashier at a pharmacy? You want more money—hey, look—there's a dollar on the ground! You want to pay off the bills—how about consolidating your credit card debt? The bills will be paid off, and now you have a new loan and payment, but you can still run those credit cards right up to the hilt again! As far as the crisis goes, now that you are out of the frying pan, how's that fire feel? And isn't it wonderful that your company is forcing you to take mandatory unpaid vacation? Now you have time to clean out the garage and have a yard sale to make up some of your lost salary! Remember the child (me) who wanted to fly for a living and ended up sitting in the back of an airliner? Fuzzy thinking yields fuzzy results.

Here's a bit of advice: Figure out what you have that you *don't* want and clearly visualize a world without it. Aim for that, and figure out what you are willing to do to obtain that world. Be a *lot* more specific than "pay off the bills"; think more along the terms of "debt-free" and having additional discretionary income and then visualize and write down what it means in terms of your home life, stress levels, and opportunities.

Once you start clearing out some of the less-than-desirable things, good things to achieve become clear. Of course, if you already are able to formulate a clear vision of a desirable future for yourself, *write it down* and get on with it!

The opening statement, "This book tells you how to achieve what you want out of life..." is done. You have everything you need to know, and more. You also have an explanation of "how it works" as well as "what to do." Knowing *how* your actions affect your outcome enables you to better apply the techniques described in chapters 8 and 9 *as well as techniques learned elsewhere.* You can set goals with better success. You can work, play, and live with more success and confidence. You should be able to understand the workings of everything you ever learned about success, even things you learned before you read this book. If you read other books on success principles, you can return to those books and understand *exactly* why those concepts work. You can even apply this to lessons you learn from religious and spiritual teachings.

This is a new way of looking at the world. You are no longer being carried along a time stream of a universe over which you have no control; instead of being carried down the river of time, you realize that every instant of your life you have a wall of open doors leading to many futures. You have the ability to choose which door (and which future) you take. Most importantly is that you know you *are* going through one door or another, *whether or not you choose*. You might as well pick the door you want!

The universe has endless possibilities. If you are a political conservative, you can choose a future where your beliefs hold sway, and the political liberal next to you can choose a future where his or her beliefs are the norm. You can do this because both continua exist, and each of you can choose which continuum you wish to observe. Oddly enough, there is no paradox to this concept. There are continua where you and I do not exist and continua where our universes never overlap. There are adjacent continua *so similar* to this continuum that they are indistinguishable except on minute examination. There are uncountable continua that are possible futures for the trajectory you are traveling. Some lead where you want to go, and some do not, and you have the ability to deliberately choose among the options.

In the previous chapter, I presented the concept that we travel along the *w* vector through multiple three-dimensional universes. In reality, we are traveling among *o, p, r, s, t, u, v, and w* vectors. There are more choices than you can possibly imagine. Fortunately, you don't need to imagine those any more than you need to be able to imagine the trillions of events that lead to raising one of your hands. You only need to be able to imagine the end result that you desire and let your consciousness choose the door that leads to those results, whether it is a hand raised in the air, a happy and healthy life, a particular car—or all three, plus much more.

Recommended Reading

I love to recommend things. In the case of books, if I particularly appreciate the skill of an author, I'll purchase a new book as soon as I see it; it's my way of showing my appreciation by using my wallet. Think of it as applause. I recommend you do the same, although any of these should be available in a good library. Following are books and individual stories from books. Everything directly mentioned in the text is in this list, as well as indirect influences. This is terribly incomplete, but I can't include everything. Because it is such an eclectic list, I've included a brief comment for each.

Abbott, Edwin. (1884). *Flatland, a Romance of Many Dimensions.* London: Seely & Co. Available online from many sources.

> Originally written as a parody on Victorian culture using two dimensional beings as characters. It is, however, a brilliant essay on the visualization of different dimensions and fun to read.

Bastiat, Frédéric. (1850). *The Law.*

> This is a discourse that makes the difference between good law and bad law (not to mention, good and bad anything) very clear. A small book that should be in everybody's library.

Carpenter, John, director. (1974). *Dark Star.* Movie.

> *Quoted in the text.* Thermostellar Bomb #20. An interesting sidebar is that Dan O'Bannon took the alien

beach ball subplot from *Dark Star* and wrote the science fiction horror classic *Alien*. I rented *Dark Star* because of that bit of information, and frankly, I preferred *Dark Star*.

Clark, Arthur C. (1962, rev. 1973). *Profiles of the Future.* New York, NY: Warner Books.

Mentioned in the text. Referencing Clark's three laws of prediction. Arthur C. Clark is a great science fiction writer who also wrote great science.

Gaiman, Neil. (1990). A Dream of a Thousand cats. In *The Sandman, Volume III (Dream Country.* New York, NY: Vertigo.

There are ten sandman graphic novels, and when I got them, they were out of print, making this the most expensive collection in my library. I'd pay it again in a heartbeat. This is my second favorite series of books, save for *The Book of the New Sun.* Fortunately for you, it is once again available. You can read *A Dream of a Thousand Cats* in a few minutes at your local bookstore, and you will see why I recommend the story. If you have any sense at all, you'll just pick up the whole set and buy them.

Greene, Brian. (1999). *The Elegant Universe, Superstrings, Hidden Dimensions, and the Quest for the Ultimate Theory.* New York, NY: Vintage Books.

A best seller and an excellent reference for the several different string theories, including their differences and how they are being reconciled through advanced mathematics.

Hill, Napoleon. (1937). *Think and grow rich.* New York, NY: Random House.

Mentioned in the text. This is the granddaddy of modern success books and still going strong. People keep adding stuff to keep it "up to date," but I have only a copy of the original. Principles are principles.

Kaku, Michio. (1994). *Hyperspace: A Scientific Odyssey Through Parallel Universes, Time Warps, and the 10th Dimension.* New York, NY: Anchor Books.

A wonderful and well-done introduction to modern physics. This is an excellent starting point for anybody interested in the subject.

Rowling, J.K. (1997). *The Harry Potter series.* New York, NY: Arthur A. Levine.

Mentioned in the text. These are just wonderful stories, and Ms. Rowling deserves every good thing that has come her way from giving us these novels.

Powers, Tim. (1983). *The Anubis Gates.* New York, NY: Ace.

Mentioned in the text. Magic candle communication.

Pratchett, Terry. (1983). *The Discworld novels.* New York, NY: HarperCollins.

Mentioned in the text. Referencing how trolls count (1, 2, many). Physics is different on the Discworld, where sunlight just oozes over the mountains and flows into the valleys. These novels range from very good to great, and are funny and insightful. Better than TV any day.

Roddenberry, Gene, creator. (1996). *Star Trek.* Television show, movies.

Mentioned in the text. Referencing Captain Picard.

Stephensen, Neil. (2008). *Anathem.* New York, NY: HarperCollins.

> Another novel written from the point of view of someone living in another continuum. Brilliantly executed with a thought-provoking view of alternate continua. Includes some really good lessons on logic and geometry.

Vanderbilt, Tom. (2008). *Traffic.* New York, NY: Alfred A. Knopf.

> *Mentioned in the text.* This should be required reading for anybody who drives a car.

***What the *bleep* do we know?* (2004)** – Movie, directed by William Arntz, Betsy Chasse, Mark Vicente.

> None of the conclusions drawn from the *physics* mentioned in the movie have anything to do with the conclusions in this book, but to be fair, it needs to be here. Quite the contrary, it was my *questioning* the conclusions of the movie that led me to the hypothesis presented here. The three-year-old stuck in my head kept saying stuff like, "Well, that bit is pretty cool, but how does that work if you have *such-and-so* going on in the universe?"
>
> Then the engineer in my head would try to figure out the answers until I finally ended up with this book. So, in a very real sense, this was the catalyst for this work; it got me thinking. Besides which, I enjoyed the movie, and the title is really a very valid question.

Wolfe, Gene. (1980). *The Book of the New Sun.* New York, NY: Tom Doherty.

> There are several books in this series. You should simply purchase and read anything by Gene Wolfe; he is *that*

good. He happens to be an engineer and thus near and dear to my heart. As an engineer, he helped invent the Pringles potato chip, and so may be near and dear to yours, too. All nerd-like bias aside, award-winning author Michael Swanwick said, "Gene Wolfe is the greatest writer in the English language alive today." You owe it to yourself to discover why he said that.

Wolfe, Gene. (1980, 2009). *Kevin Malone* (short story, 1980). From the collection, *The Best of Gene Wolfe*. New York, Toronto: Macmillan.

Mentioned in the text. Referencing "free wealth."

Glossary

All definitions below represent the words or phrases as used in this book, and are not intended to replace dictionary definitions. Use in everyday conversation at your own risk.

ana—ΕΠάνω—Greek for "up." The term coined by Charles Hinton in the late nineteenth century to specify one of the directions in the fourth spatial dimension.

believe—To regard as true.

Big Boy Warranty—I once bought a modem for an HP-1000 computer with the RTE-IV operating system (this was back in the olden days). The modem did not come with a driver and would not work without one. HP provided a text file with an example driver written in macro code. In the file was a warranty statement commented in the banner that read something like this: *"This example code is intended to help you and is covered exclusively by our Big Boy Warranty. The Big Boy Warranty states: You need to modify this to make it work on your system. If you do so, and it does not work, You Are A Big Boy Now; Fix It Yourself."*

Life comes with a Big Boy Warranty. It's got nothing to do with this book, but I thought I'd toss it in for free.

Bomb #20—The planet-busting, thermostellar bomb that is a central character on the interstellar ship Dark Star in a movie of the same name.

brane (*n*-brane, 1-brane, 2-brane, etc.)—By definition, an extended object having any number of dimensions rather than just one dimension. Used in the text to describe a point of view (or world) that is bound by a specific number of dimensions, such as a line (1-brane) or plane (2-brane).

bundle—Continua that are spatially close and very similar to one another. It is conceivable that your consciousness can influence your path so that you experience a continuum that is in accordance with your desires. Because your consciousness is limited in its ability to deflect your path, continua that are more spatially separated from your current path will take longer to reach than continua in your immediate proximity (bundle).

c-**quota**—My phrase to illustrate the movement of matter through all dimensions as described by Einstein in his theory of special relativity. All matter travels at this speed all of the time. Light achieves this velocity moving in one dimension, so it is best known as the speed of light. Best known as the "*c*" in the famous formula $E=mc^2$. Spatially, we are relatively at rest compared to a photon, and so we use most of our quota traveling the dimension we imagine as time.

Calabi-Yau manifold—In supersymmetric string theory, the mathematically consistent shape into which the extra dimensions are rolled up. There is no limit to the number of dimensions that can be in a Calabi-Yau manifold.

casting—To figuratively cast a spell in which you write down the desired result, the payment given, who it affects, and when it will occur.

continua—The plural for continuum.

continuum—A universe in continuous motion, or continuous motion through many universes. In your case, the universe in which you live.

dendritic—Branching, like a tree. In the case of neurons, it is as though the neuron is the trunk of the tree, and each tip of every branch is attached to a different neuron.

diabolical mechanism—One of the more interesting ways to skin a cat.

$e=mc^2$—Albert Einstein's equation representing mass–energy equivalence: e represents energy, m represents mass, and c represents the speed of light in a vacuum. Writing this equation as $e/m=c^2$ clearly shows the proportional relationship of mass to energy.

equivalence—Einstein stated: "... *the law of the equality of the inertial and gravitational mass is equivalent to the assertion that the acceleration imparted to a body by a gravitational field is independent of the nature of the body.*" Basically, the action of gravity on a body is exactly the same as accelerating the body in the absence of gravity. In this text, the effect of the observer's point of view moving past objects, or objects moving past the observer's point of view, are equivalent, and that equivalence is used to propose the condition that we, as observers, are moving through multiple *3*-brane universes, as opposed to remaining in a single four dimensional universe that is constantly changing.

evil aliens—Millions of people believe the souls of these possess mankind and cause us to do bad things (see season 9, episode 12 of *South Park*). That you are a being traveling through the multidimensional universe is far more believable and costs a lot less money.

foreigner—You would not be able to understand a single thought from the mind of one of these people even if you were fully telepathic.

general relativity—Also known as the theory of general relativity, was published in 1915 by Albert Einstein. This unified Newton's law of gravitation with Einstein's own theory of special relativity, published in 1905. As it applies here, Einstein's equivalence principle is introduced in general relativity.

Heisenberg uncertainty principle—In quantum mechanics, certain pairs of properties cannot be known with precision; the precise measurement of one property will proportionally reduce the precision of the other. The most common pair is location and momentum. If you fix the location of the particle, you are less able to determine the momentum, and vice versa.

I AM—From Exodus 3:14, in which the phrase, "I Am that I Am" is God's response when Moses asked his name. I AM was used as the name of sanctuaries and temples of the St. Germain foundation, which gave birth to many New Age spiritual movements. Every August, there is an "'I AM' Come!" festival in Mount Shasta, California.

inertia—The property of matter that resists change in its existing state of rest or motion.

infinite—A term that represents a number without end, or a number so large that it would appear to be so.

kata—Κάτω από – Greek for "Down." The term coined by Charles Hinton in the late nineteenth century to specify one of the directions in the fourth spatial dimension.

magic—An observable phenomenon that you cannot explain with your existing knowledge. The amount of physics you know has a lot to do with how much magic you see around you.

miracle—Given that we are, as author Desmond Morris once pointed out, simply a naked ape, a miracle is anything that is really amazing when you stop to think about it for a minute. Your clothes, for instance; without them, you'd pretty much be stuck living in a warm, shady place where food grew out of the ground. You could completely forget about, say, New York or Chicago.

paradigm—The pattern or model for the basis of theory or belief.

photon—An elementary particle that has energy and movement but does not have mass or electrical charge. It is how all forms of electromagnetic radiation are transmitted. In a vacuum, photons travel at the speed of light along one vector.

physics—The study of nature, with a particular focus on matter and energy.

Planck length—Approximately 1.616252×10^{-35} meters as listed by the National Institute of Standards and Technology (NIST). This is the approximate size of a string in string theory.

psychology—The study of the human mind.

quantum mechanics—A mathematical description of reality at the atomic and subatomic level following the discovery that particles are discrete packets of energy with wave-like properties.

quantum superposition—In quantum mechanics, quantum superposition is the sum of all of the possible states of a particle, creating a complex probability wave in space where the most likely position of a particle is at the peaks of the waveform. If an observer locates a particle, the waveform collapses to one state at the time of observation but exists in all states until then.

quark—A fundamental building block of matter, the several different types of quark are components of hadrons. The most familiar hadrons are protons and neutrons. Quarks are always bound to other quarks in nature and are not found in isolation.

Schrödinger's cat—The famous thought experiment posed by physicist Erwin Schrödinger in 1935 to illustrate the paradox of quantum superposition. In the experiment, you would place a cat in a box with a *diabolical mechanism* that consisted of a small bit of radioactive material, a Geiger counter, a relay, a small hammer, and a sealed flask with hydrocyanic acid. It was rigged up in such a way that perhaps in the course of a day, a radioactive particle would trigger the Geiger counter that would then trigger the relay, in turn releasing the hammer that would break the flask, release the poison, and kill the cat. According to quantum superposition, the radioactive material is in both states (decayed, not decayed) until it is measured; therefore, the cat must be both alive and dead until you open the box and look, at which point it is one or the other.

spacetime—Since the advent of Einstein's theory of relativity, time is now considered to be just another dimension equivalent to length, width, and height. Therefore, the description of a location of our universe is considered to be a location in spacetime, not just space. In mainstream media, you can see the use of the term "spacetime" as the subtitle to the documentary, "Cosmos, a Spacetime Odyssey."

special relativity—Albert Einstein proposed what is now known as special relativity or the theory of special relativity in the 1905 paper entitled "On the Electrodynamics of Moving Bodies." He states that there is no absolute state of rest or privileged reference frames and postulated that the speed of light is the same for all observers regardless of the motion of the source. As it applies here, it states that time is a fourth dimension and is not fixed; as we increase our relative speed relative to a "stationary" observer, the ticking of our watch will appear to slow down to the observer, although it will remain the same for us. Time and space can each vary for different observers, but spacetime is constant.

speed of light—This would be more accurately called the speed of everything or the speed of energy. A photon of light travels in one dimension, so all of its speed is consumed traveling in that single dimension. There is no time on a photon, because in order for what we call time to exist, we must travel in more than one dimension, and thus divert a portion of that speed to those other dimensions.

subconscious or unconscious mind—The part of your mind that does things with your body when you aren't watching, like digesting food and beating your heart. This is the action of the brain that maintains autonomous motor functions, instincts, and learned behaviors. Many authors use the subconscious mind to explain the otherwise magical results of various success principles.

success—if you are happy with your life, and happy about the direction you are headed, then you have achieved success. Not to be confused with contentment; you can be very happy with your current situation and still have a desire to achieve even greater success.

success principles—things that you can do that will increase your chances of achieving success in any endeavor.

superstring theory—Short for supersymmetric string theory. Reference to a collection of modern string theories that state as a premise that the fundamental building block of mass and energy (the same thing, remember) is a vibrating loop of string.

TANSTAAFL—Coined by Robert Heinlein, the acronym of *"There Ain't No Such Thing As A Free Lunch."*

technology—Magic, to the uninitiated.

time—Pretty much the same thing as space according to this book, the theory of relativity, and other works. An interesting definition is that the past is something that can signal an observer, and the future is something an observer can signal.

universe—All of existence.

universal consciousness—Because time is a dimension, if we measure backward along our continuum, we will eventually merge with our mother, who will merge with hers, and so on back to the beginning of consciousness. Moving forward, our consciousness will branch into every future continuum. Following this logic, we are all one, huge, interconnected universal consciousness. It makes a certain amount of sense, but I still can't figure out what the foreigner is thinking.

virtual, virtually—Not Real. Not Really. I'm throwing this in for free, too, because in today's world of technology, nearly everything is "virtual." If you replace the word "virtual" with the words "not real," life makes a lot more sense. For example, "virtually done" becomes "not really done." "It's a virtual bonanza" becomes "it's not a real bonanza." "Virtual memory" becomes "not real memory." "We're virtually giving the entire store away!" becomes "we're not really giving the entire store away!" and so on. This little tidbit alone is worth the price of the book.

***w*-vector, *w*-axis**—Motion through three dimensions is described as motion along the x, y, and z axes. Motion through a fourth dimension (time, for example) is described as motion along the w axis. Motion through additional axes counts down alphabetically from "w".

Acknowledgements

Five years ago, *The Physics of Success* was a draft manuscript that went out to family and friends, who returned comments, suggestions, corrections, and most importantly, asked a lot of questions. So, many thanks to my daughter Jennifer who started this whole process, my brother Anthony (who also contributed to *this* manuscript), John Parsons, Laurie Corbin, and Christine Zimmerman. Without your help getting the book off the ground, this second edition would not exist.

Sammy the bread-stealing cat is still making me laugh every day. He was able to assist even more this time because even a cat can work a touch screen. I'm blaming any errors on the cat.

For this edition, many thanks to Steve Harrison and his team at Bradley Communications. In particular, Martha Bullen who very patiently kept poking and prodding at me until I sat down and rewrote the book. She was right—it was worth it. She also introduced me to Madalyn Stone, who edited the book you have in your hands. It was quite an overhaul, and the book is immeasurably better because of her valuable input.

And of course, without the patient tolerance of Andrea Chasez, listening to these ideas over a period of years, always offering amazing advice and incredible support, none of this would have happened. She is, without the slightest doubt, not only the best part of my world, but the best part of me.

Front Cover Image

Gas plume from a newborn star in the Orion Nebula, taken by the Hubble Space Telescope's Wide Field and Planetary Camera on August 13 and 14, 1991.

ABOUT THE AUTHOR

Michael Ciarochi began working as an engineer and surveyor in his home state of Alaska, where he worked on the design and construction of the trans-Alaska pipeline for several years. He later became involved in mining and metallurgical plant design, working on mines from Sweden to the South Pacific. When computer-aided design (CAD) became practical, he applied his talent in that field as a consultant to assist engineering companies in making the successful transition from paper to electronic media. Subsequently, he worked directly for large technology companies in service delivery to major global corporations, specializing in networks, information security, and cryptography.

Originally trained as a musician, Michael still plays trumpet and bass with various groups in the Atlanta, Georgia area. He supports his habit by working with individuals, groups, and corporations to help them set and achieve their goals through the principles set forth in *The Physics of Success*.

Learn more at
http://www.ThePhysicsOfSuccess.com